IMAGES
of America
INDIO

ON THE COVER: As Indio, California, developed, it became known as the "Date Capital of the United States." The regal date palms, transplanted from the Middle East and North Africa, dominated the landscape and invited permanent residents and tourists to enjoy their shade and delicious fruit. Two of Indio's best-known retail date shops were in Sniff's Date Gardens, shown here, and Shield's Date Gardens, famous for its slide show entitled "The Romance and Sex Life of the Date." (Courtesy of the Coachella Valley Historical Society.)

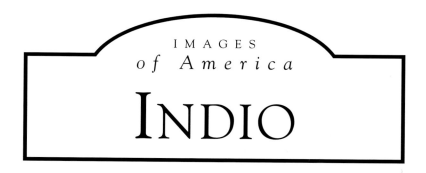

IMAGES of America
INDIO

Patricia Baker Laflin
for the Coachella Valley Historical Society

Copyright © 2008 by Patricia Baker Laflin and the Coachella Valley Historical Society
ISBN 978-0-7385-5618-5

Published by Arcadia Publishing
Charleston SC, Chicago IL, Portsmouth NH, San Francisco CA

Printed in the United States of America

Library of Congress Catalog Card Number: 2007936201

For all general information contact Arcadia Publishing at:
Telephone 843-853-2070
Fax 843-853-0044
E-mail sales@arcadiapublishing.com
For customer service and orders:
Toll-Free 1-888-313-2665

Visit us on the Internet at www.arcadiapublishing.com

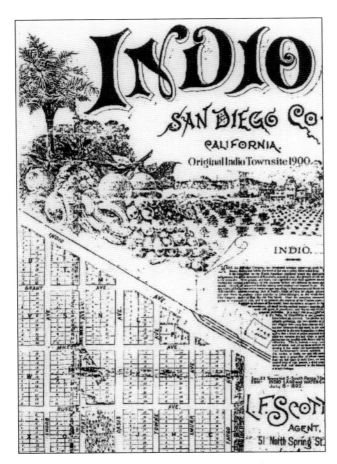

Although this early map of the Indio town site is dated 1900, the original was done in 1892 when the Coachella Valley was a part of San Diego County. In 1893, the huge county was divided, and this desert region became a part of the newly created Riverside County.

Contents

Acknowledgments		6
Introduction		7
1.	Indio's First People	9
2.	The Southern Pacific Railroad Arrives	15
3.	Creating a Community	27
4.	Indio Was a Mining Town	77
5.	World War II Changed Indio	91
6.	Water Shaped Development	103
7.	Parades, Pageants, Festivals, and Fun	111

Acknowledgments

The Coachella Valley Historical Society, successor to the Coachella Valley Pioneer's Society, is responsible for the collection and preservation of the photographs and memories presented in this book. The pioneer society dreamed of establishing a museum—the historical society made it happen in 1984—and their museum archives have made this book possible. It is difficult to name all of the volunteers whose work this book represents, but first and foremost I should mention Ole Nordland, editor of the *Indio Daily News* for many years and later secretary of the Coachella Valley Water District. Ole collected pictures and articles about many phases of the valley's life and left to the museum a filing cabinet full of treasures. He added water district photographs to the museum collection. He also authored *Coachella Valley's Golden Years*, a source book for many writers since its first publication in 1968. Otho Moore and Ruth White Peters lived here in Indio's early days, and both gave to the museum a wealth of pictures and information. Dorothy Schmid, Geri Robertson, Margaret Tyler, and Connie Cowan faithfully identified pictures and memorabilia. Mention should also be made of my husband, Ben Laflin, who supported my many hours of research and writing, and contributed his own memories of early days in the valley. All photographs in this book, unless otherwise noted, are from the archives of the Coachella Valley Historical Society located in Indio.

INTRODUCTION

The story of Indio is the story of one of America's last frontiers—a story that began just a little over 100 years ago. Indio is located in the Coachella Valley in California's southeastern corner, an area originally deemed totally unsuitable for settlement. It was called the Salton Sink, and it was the nemesis of many overland travelers until the railroad built tracks through its apparently arid waste. Passengers traveling through could see that plants grew well along the railroad right-of-way. Those early steam engines needed a lot of water, and the Southern Pacific had the improved well-drilling equipment needed to reach the water that lay in the abundant aquifer under the center of the valley. The surface was a desert only because it lacked water. The reclamation of this land is one of the great success stories of the 20th century.

Geographic location was the single most deciding factor in the establishment of the city of Indio. Indio's first inhabitants were Cahuilla Indians who lived in a winter village they called Paltewat in the shade of the native fan palms. The palms, one of the very few groups in the center of the desert, meant available water—essential to life in this very arid land. The Cahuilla regularly migrated to the western mountains in the summer, and in the winter, they sought out those palm oases in the warm valley floor.

The Cahuilla hunter-gatherer lifestyle changed forever with the arrival of the work crews building the Southern Pacific Railroad through the Coachella Valley—the last link in the southern transcontinental railroad. Indio was first known as Indian Wells and was located exactly halfway between Los Angeles and Yuma. It was the logical place to establish a division point. The U.S. government's generous gift of alternate sections of land to the Southern Pacific Railroad meant that the natives could no longer roam freely. Reservations were established, and the native people became the first work force in the settlement of the valley. They really had no choice but to take those jobs.

Discovering that "Indian Wells" already appeared on government maps as a place five or six miles to the west where there was a "walk-in" well and a camping spot, the railroad chose the name of Indio for their town. The Cahuilla village site became known as Apostle Palms, since there were 12 palms at that location. Water was piped from the palm oasis to the tiny town of Indio.

Life in Indio centered around the railroad depot. It was the area's only hotel and restaurant, serving train passengers and crews, and the townspeople. There were no good roads, only dusty trails through the sand dunes, and most of the early residents lived close to the tracks. In 1896, Indio had 50 inhabitants, mostly men. There were a few storekeepers, but most worked for the railroad. Supplies came in by train or along the Bradshaw Trail, which hugged the base of the western mountains to avoid the treacherous sand of the central valley. Inventing ways to stay cool in the blistering summer heat, the settlers were most creative. Homes had double roofs, and "submarines" were sleeping rooms where water ran slowly down through burlap, reducing the inside temperature by as much as 20 degrees. People helped each other. An amazing amount of culture was provided by the pioneer women when they arrived, making sure that music, literature, and good schooling were available. Indio was literally one of the country's last frontier towns. Its citizens voted to incorporate in 1930, making it the Coachella Valley's first incorporated city.

Indio was a mining town in the 1930s when the biggest construction project in the United States during those Depression years was being executed in the mountains east of the city. The Metropolitan Aqueduct, built to carry water to the Los Angeles Basin from the Colorado River, involved 92 miles of tunnels through the eastern mountains. Indio was the center for supplies and for rest and recreation for the hard-rock mining crews, and business boomed.

World War II followed on the heels of the aqueduct project. Gen. George Patton selected land east of Indio for his desert training camp, preparing troops for the North Africa campaign. Camp Young was established about 25 miles to the east of the city, and Indio became the supply depot and host to over 75,000 soldiers needing rest and recreation. Many of those service personnel came back with their families to live in the valley after the war.

Indio experienced new life and growth with the arrival of irrigation water from the Colorado River upon the completion of the Coachella Branch of the All-American Canal. This was all a part of the Boulder Dam project. Indio became a shipping point for the valley's agricultural bounty, as well as a center for many of the new farms. It advertised itself as the Date Capital of the World. This was a slight exaggeration, but it was truly the date capital of the United States.

With this claim to fame established, the Riverside County Fair and National Date Festival became an annual event enthusiastically supported by Indio's businesses and citizens. People dressed in Arabian costumes for the fair's 10-day run, and visitors flocked to the permanent fair grounds in Indio. A nightly Arabian Nights pageant was a feature of the celebration each year.

In the 1930s and 1940s, Western Days celebrations were popular, and in recent years, other festivals have been added to the city calendar. One of the most successful has been the annual Tamale Festival in December. Indio, in 2007, is growing rapidly. Air-conditioning has made the summer heat very bearable, and people are flocking to the desert—glad to leave the snow, hurricanes, and tornados for nine months of very comfortable weather and three months or so that can be endured thanks to modern technology. People came to recover their health in a warm, dry climate in Indio's early days, and many come for the same reason today. Today's residents and visitors are curious to know how those early settlers conquered the desert, and Indio's story is worth retelling today.

One

INDIO'S FIRST PEOPLE

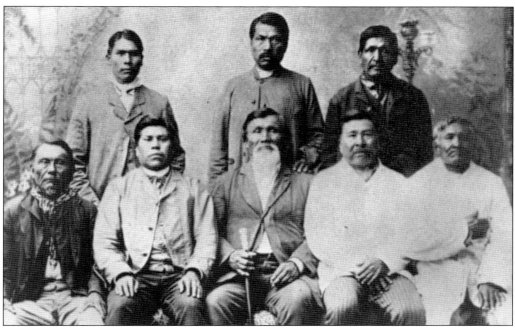

Indio is the Spanish word for Indian. The name for the new town was appropriate because Native Americans had been living in and around the site for many years. The desert Cahuilla Indians were able to establish villages out in the floor of the Coachella Valley because of ingenious dug wells called "walk-in" wells. Wherever there was a seep or weak spring, they would dig a long, narrow, open passageway with steps or a ramp leading down to the water source—usually within 15 or 30 feet of the surface. Descendants of these people, thought to have lived in the valley for at least 900 years, are pictured in this 1920 photograph. They are, from left to right, (first row) Captains Labiel, Will Pablo, Manuel, and Jose Maria; (second row) Captains Roman, Jim, and Sastro. Seated in the center of the first row is Chief Cabazon. Chemehuevi people also lived in the valley, traveling from traditional lands near the Colorado River to meet, trade, and hunt with the desert Cahuillas.

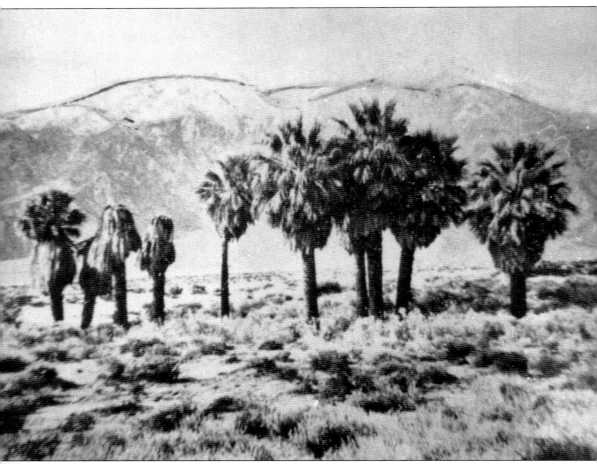

Thought to be the only native palm oasis in the middle of the Coachella Valley, Apostle Palms was so named by an early survey party because there were 12 palms at this site of a well and an ancient Native American village. Railroad surveyors were quick to realize that this water source, located within a few miles of the planned midway point on the Yuma–to–Los Angeles segment of the line, would be very valuable to railroad building crews and to the future settlement. Water was hauled and piped to the new town from this oasis. Railroad officials originally planned to call the division point Indian Wells, but it was discovered that the area just west of their new town was already designated by that name on existing maps, so they settled for Indio. It was an appropriate choice, honoring the valley's original inhabitants. The palms burned shortly after this 1912 photograph was taken, and the logs that could be salvaged were used to build a house on the nearby dirt road, which became Washington Street.

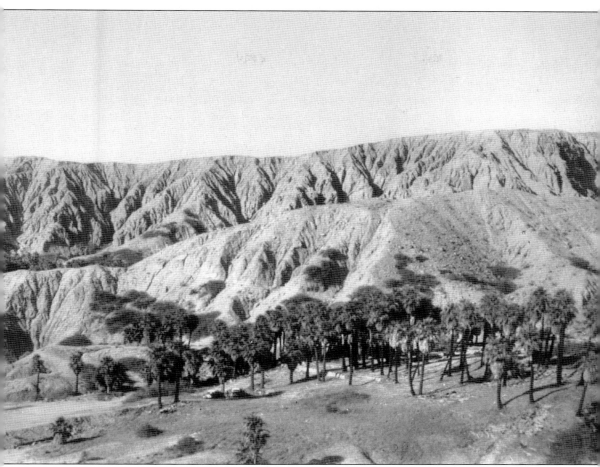

Most of the Native American villages were located at the base of the mountains on both sides of the valley. Water was available near the surface wherever these native palms grew, and not only could the natives use the water, but the palms also provided both food and shelter during the winter months. In the summer, the natives moved up the western mountains to cooler campsites. This is Biskra Palms, located atop the San Andreas Fault three miles northeast of Indio. It has been a location for movies, including *Tripoli* and *Ten Tall Men*. In 1929, there was an ambitious plan to develop "the Walled City of Biskra" here, including an expensive hotel, narrow streets, and shops reminiscent of a Saharan village. Expensive private estates would be built outside the city walls. Busloads of prospective buyers came from Los Angeles and were served meals catered by an Indio restaurant in a huge tent. Unfortunately the stockholders of the Biskra Trust went down with the market crash of 1929, leaving only a few roads and stone terraces as a reminder of their idea.

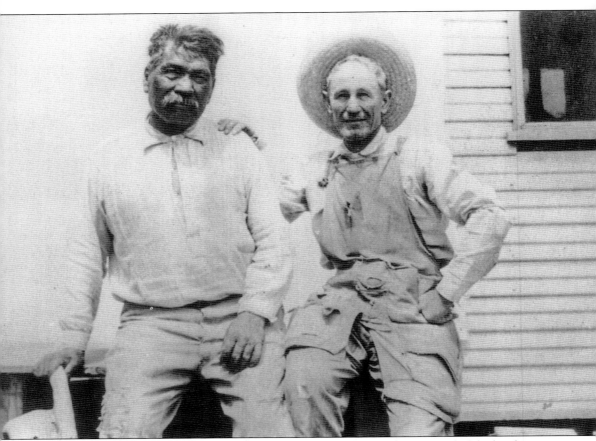

Captain Jim (left), shown here with early settler Jessie Rice Pearson, was typical of the local natives who worked with the settlers to develop the valley. The Native Americans were deprived of their traditional hunter-gatherer lifestyle when the U.S. government gave alternate sections of their land to the railroad as an inducement to construction. The railroad sold land to the settlers and so did the government. After 1876, the native people were allotted reservations much too small to support families used to roaming the entire valley and the mountains for game and plant foods. They were very hardworking and reliable, and were employed by the railroad, local farmers, and at the salt works located in the lake bed of the dry Salton Sea.

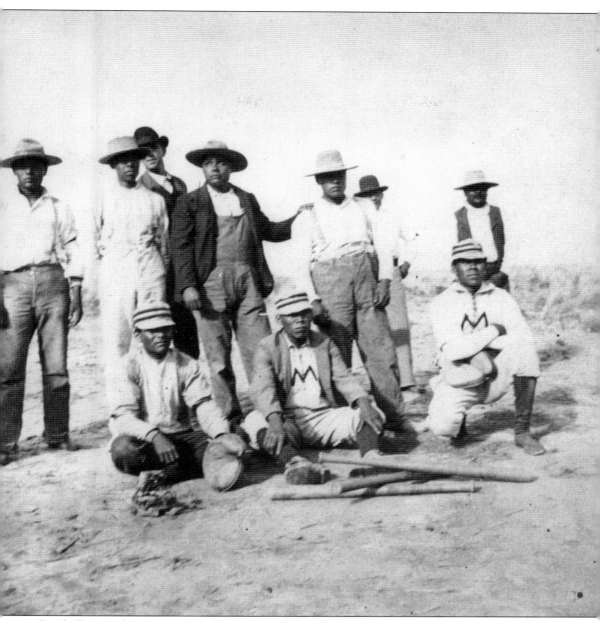

Baseball was a favorite pastime for white settlers and Native Americans alike. Pictured here is an early Indio Native American team. A similar team in Coachella, made up mostly of native athletes, was a league champion in 1914, and it sent players to a tournament in Japan. They traveled, of course, by ship, and it was a fairly lengthy trip. The newspapers made much of their travels and their successes.

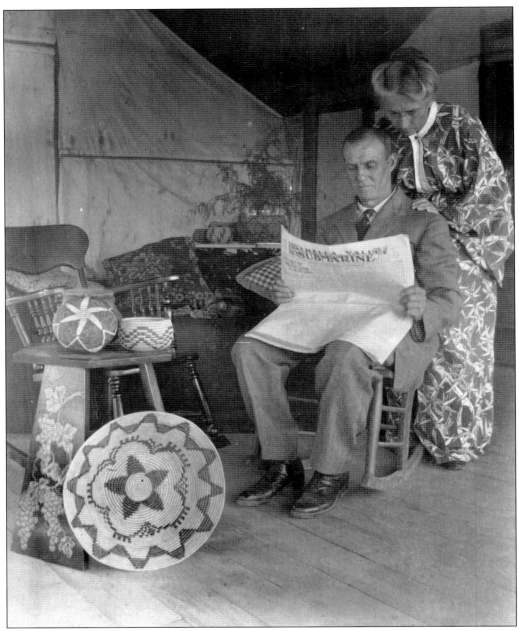
Early Indio residents James and Elizabeth Moore are shown with several of their beautiful Native American baskets. Both the Cahuilla and Chemehuevi women were noted for the exceptional quality of their baskets. Unlike many other tribes, they sewed their baskets with willow and other plant fiber.

Two

THE SOUTHERN PACIFIC RAILROAD ARRIVES

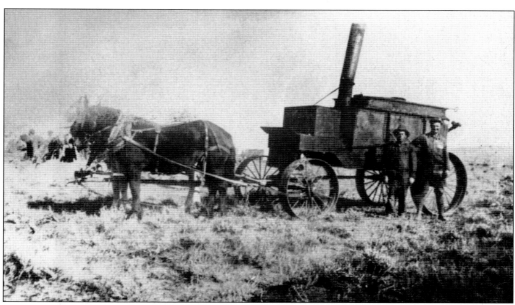

There was no white settlement at Indio until the railroad arrived in 1876. A railroad survey party had located a route through the center of the valley in 1872, and thereafter, work crews labored to grade and build up a roadbed. Today we take trains for granted, but building and maintaining tracks through the desert was not easy. Frequent cloudbursts washed out the newly graded route. Culverts and riprap of rocks were necessary to protect the grade from the floods rushing out of the canyons. A new hazard, blow sand, filled the tracks, and the sharp sand particles cut off telegraph poles. A special section crew had to shovel sand out of tracks and switches as the tracks inched toward Indio. This horse-drawn cook wagon served the crews surveying and building the railroad.

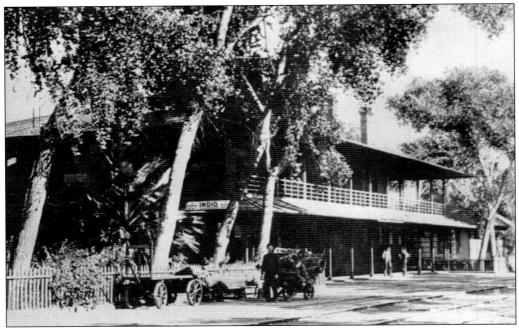

These two views show the first permanent building in Indio, the Southern Pacific Depot Hotel. Several maintenance buildings were constructed prior to the completion of the depot in 1879 or 1880. Passengers dined here while the train stopped for 20 minutes on both its eastern and western journey. It was also the center of social life in the community of Indio, which was developing alongside the tracks. There was a limited number of hotel rooms available on the second floor. Trains furnished the most reliable way to travel to the other new towns springing up to the south. A local train called "The Sidewinder" made two runs a day, and it was possible to commute between Indio and Mecca to a job or for shopping.

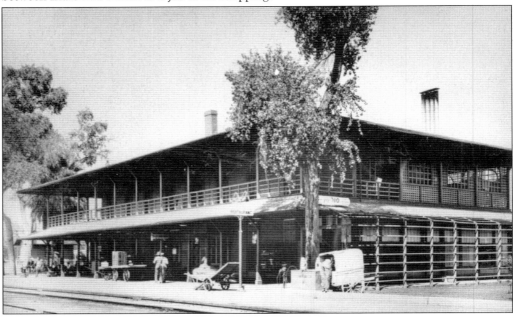

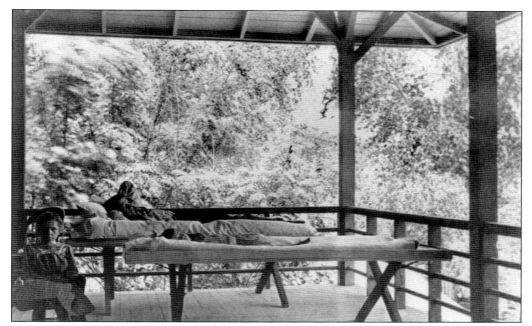

Cots were moved out onto the second-floor porch of the depot during the summer, affording a cooler alternative to the bedrooms. Here the children of the hotel managers enjoy the fresh air. Trees and shrubs are also a cooling influence.

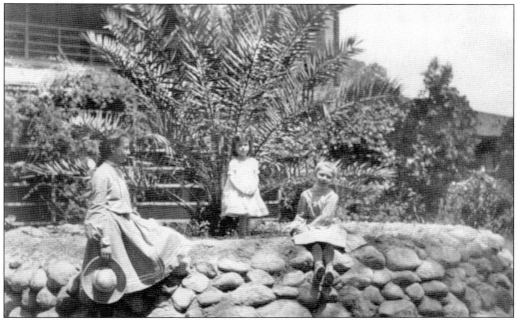

Pictured from left to right, Marguerite, Lucia, and Frances Ford pose in the garden area on the east side of the hotel in 1907. The railroad intentionally planted attractive gardens near their stations, hoping to influence travelers to think about purchasing land and moving to the desert. Since the railroad had to sell the land it had been given by the government to make a profit, this was smart marketing on their part.

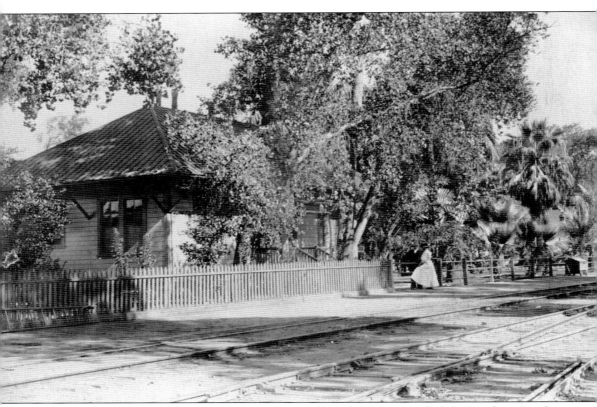

The Southern Pacific Railroad built this infirmary about 1897. It was called the Southern Pacific Hospital by the locals, but it really was just a clinic for the railroad workers and their families. There was a nurse on duty, but anyone suffering a serious accident or illness was given emergency treatment and then put on the next train going west toward Los Angeles or San Bernardino, the closest real hospitals. Because of the use of kerosene or coal oil lamps and stoves and the fact that all of the buildings were frame structures, there were many fires, and burn victims rarely survived. The Southern Pacific furnished the only real firefighting equipment for the young settlement. They had 1,000 feet of fire hose attached to their pumps. If the structure fire was within reach of that hose, there was a chance to save the building. Otherwise they had to depend on a bucket brigade, and that was rarely effective in quelling the blaze.

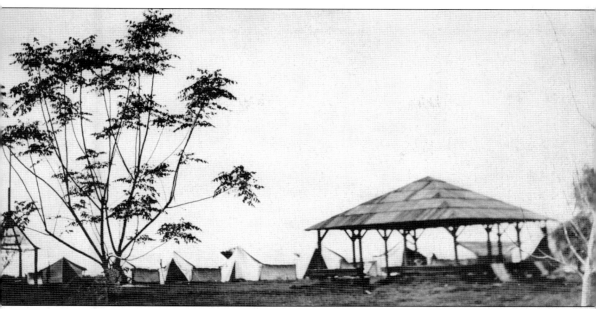

In 1903, N. O. Nelson, a Chicago philanthropist, opened what was called the Indio Health Camp on land adjoining the depot. It consisted of a number of tents and tent houses set 20 feet apart, open to permit air to circulate. Tuberculosis was rampant at the beginning of the 20th century, and there were no drugs with which to treat patients. Eastern doctors could only suggest that warm, dry air might be beneficial. Trains brought the hopeful victims to Indio. The 60-acre plot was planted with vegetables and other produce, and in need of a farm manager when Dr. June Robertson and her husband, John, arrived in 1904. John had tuberculosis but was initially able to work and was given the manager's job. Dr. June was begged to become the camp doctor and eventually the doctor for the entire Coachella Valley. An early valley cemetery was located near the camp on north Jackson Street—a sad reminder that tuberculosis was tough to conquer.

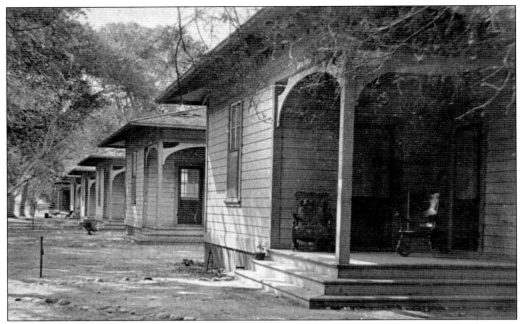

By 1907, this very respectable row of employee houses was in use by the train master, depot agent, road foreman, and other supervisory personnel. They were located on the south side of the tracks, just south of the present Jackson Street overpass. The tall, native California fan palms along Indio Boulevard still stand at the site.

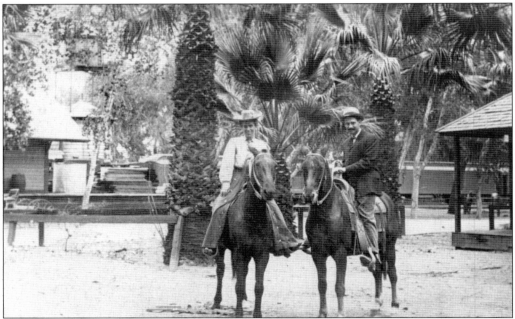

On the back of this 1908 real photo postcard, Grace Dixon wrote, "In Indio, Brother Howard and I on our pet ponies, Fred and Bill." A railroad baggage car is visible in the background. The shady grounds around the depot made the area very attractive to local residents and to the train passengers passing through.

Railroad workers identified as Mr. McIntyre and Mr. Kuhl enjoyed a bit of tennis on the court behind the cottages. Notice the double roof on the building. This was a common style of construction because the air space between the two roofs helped keep the rooms cooler in the summer heat. This photograph is labeled "Before 1910."

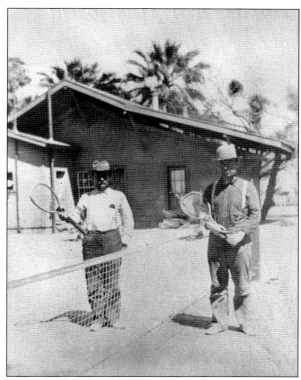

The proximity of the cottages to the railroad tracks is shown in this view looking from the depot toward the Indio settlement. These tall cottonwood trees have obviously been here 20 or 25 years, probably having been planted when the depot was first built. Desert dwellers appreciated shade and recognized its lifesaving value.

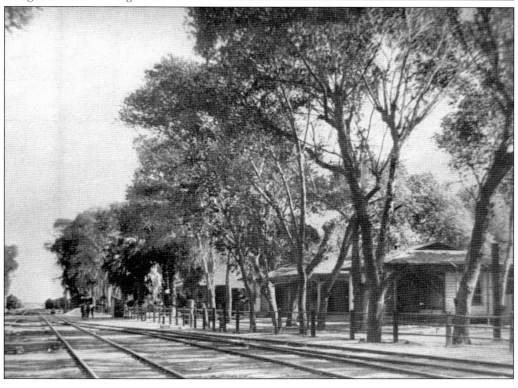

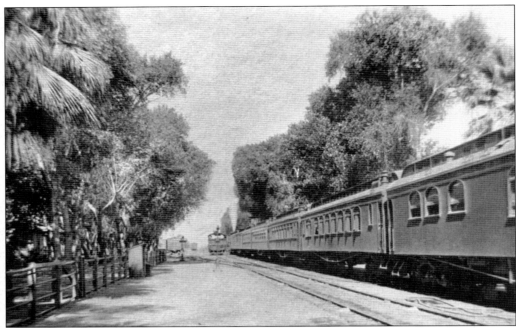

This 1907 photograph pictures a passenger train stopped in the Indio rail yard. These trains regularly served the desert area. Interestingly, in the early days, there were sometimes mixed trains of passenger and freight cars, the latter bringing a family's livestock and farm equipment from the Midwest to this new frontier.

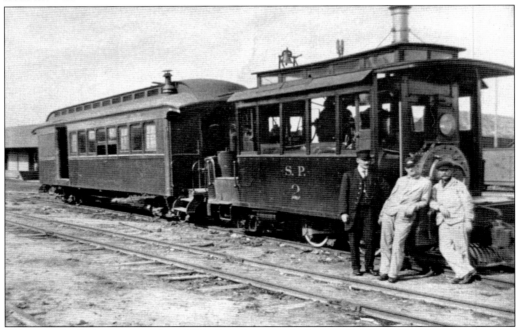

Taken in the Indio train yard in 1903, this photograph shows a Southern Pacific inspection car and coach, and railroad employees Rearford, Foresight, and Williamson. Indio was the hub of maintenance work on the desert section of the line.

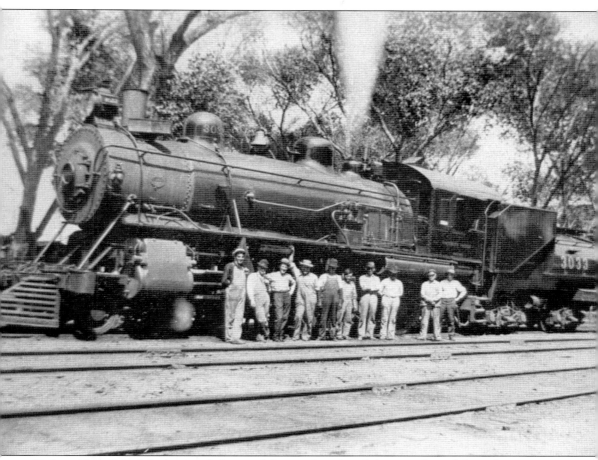

Early resident Otho Moore provided most of these early railroad photographs and the information that accompanies them. In this 1912 photograph, he calls this the "Fast Passenger Engine 3033 in the Indio SP Yards." Among those pictured are, from left to right, Fieldmiller, Lee "Kid," unidentified, Frank Runyon, unidentified, a Japanese rail worker, and Lewis Marsh. The photographs of Otho Moore and his parents, James and Elizabeth Moore, provide a priceless record of the early days in the Coachella Valley.

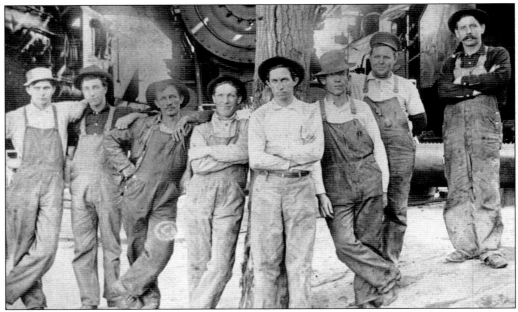

The Southern Pacific Railroad was the principal employer of Indio residents when this 1914 photograph was taken in front of the roundhouse. Some were single men living in Southern Pacific housing, but most were family men living across the tracks in the developing city. These crews kept the steam engines and cars in good repair.

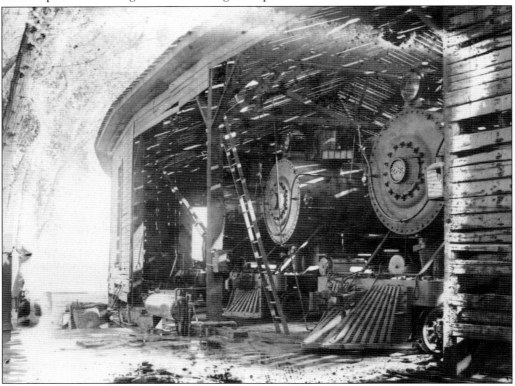

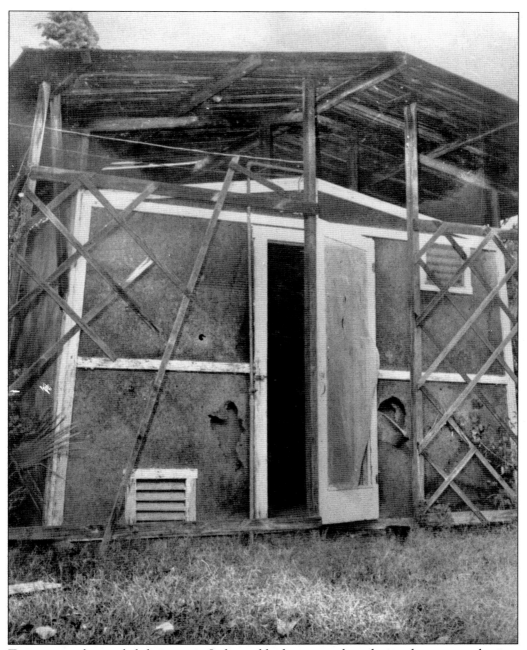

Train crews often ended their run in Indio and had to try to sleep during the extreme daytime heat in summer. This is a sleeping room called a "submarine," invented by a railroad worker. It was a small room faced with beaverboard and covered with a shade over the roof. A water pipe crossed the roof. The pipe dripped water, which ran down the burlap-covered sides of the building, evaporating as it did so and cooling the interior of the room by as much as 20 degrees. The room was large enough to contain a cot, a small dresser, a table, and a chair.

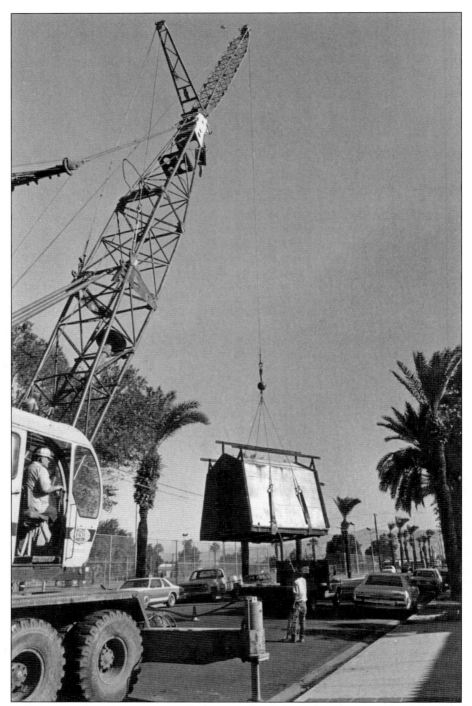
Almost 100 years after its invention, a "submarine" is delivered to the grounds of the Coachella Valley Museum and Cultural Center in 1987. The small size of these sleeping rooms is evident in this photograph. It made the trip safely and can be seen on the museum grounds in Indio—a graphic reminder of the ingenuity of those early residents.

Three
CREATING A COMMUNITY

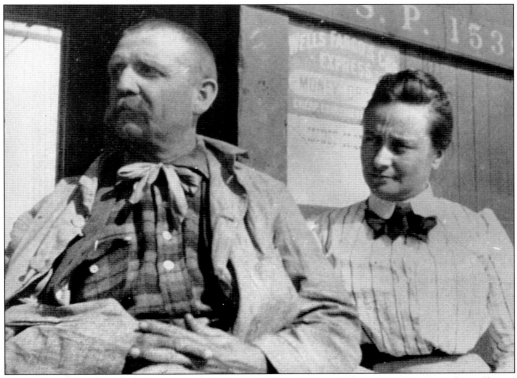

A. G. Tingman, shown here with his wife, is called "the Father of Indio." He came to the valley as a railroad construction boss in 1877 and became telegrapher and station agent in 1883. He built Indio's first store northwest of the depot in 1885 and became Indio's first postmaster on July 3, 1888. This was the second post office in the valley, the first being located near Palm Springs in the area now occupied by Smoke Tree Ranch. He homesteaded and laid out the original town site, drilled a well for his home and store, and built a corral for travelers, prospectors, and freighters. He obviously caught the gold bug because he sold his store in 1903 and devoted himself to prospecting until his death at the Full Moon Mine, north of Niland, in 1925.

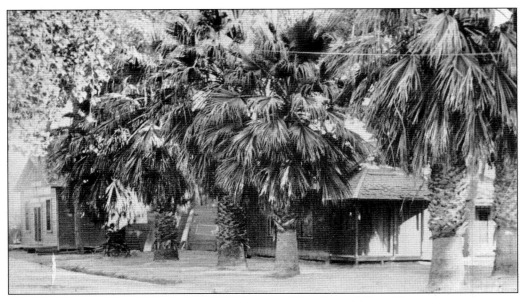

The home and store of Indio pioneer merchant and developer Albert Tingman are shown in this photograph believed to have been taken in 1900. The store is on the left and the home on the right under the fan palms. The buildings were situated in what would now be the middle of Indio Boulevard, east of Fargo Street and north of Bliss Street.

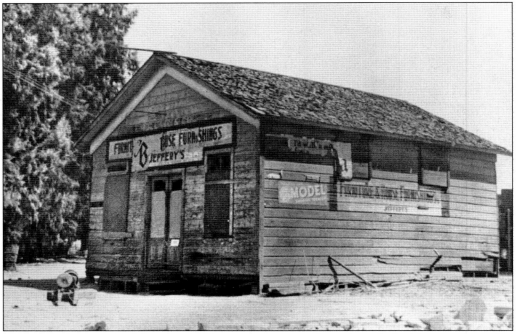

This 1938 photograph of the original Tingman store was taken when the building was moved to eliminate a bottleneck in Indio Boulevard, known at that time as Highway 99. It had been the first home of the *Indio Date Palm* newspaper and the Jeffery Furniture Store.

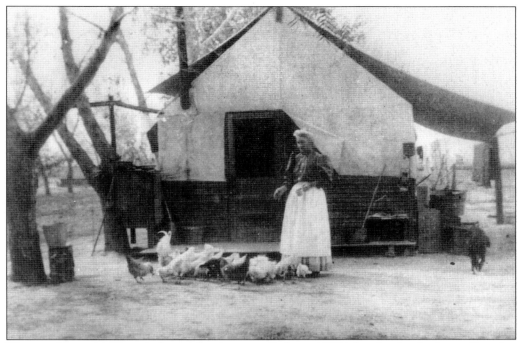

This tent house was typical of many first homes in Indio in 1907. Most families had a small garden and chickens to provide fresh meat and vegetables. Staple groceries could be ordered from Ralph Grocery Company in Los Angeles. They were delivered by train.

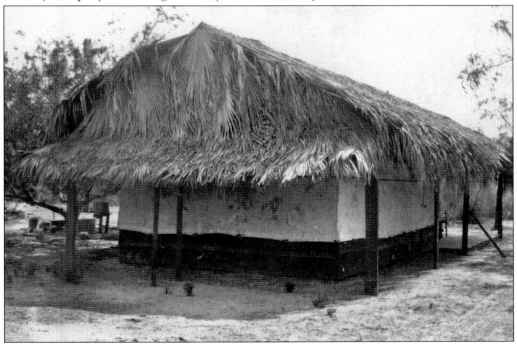

Relief from the extreme summer heat was afforded by a palm-leaf structure built to completely cover the tent house. This was the home of pioneers James and Elizabeth Moore from 1907 to 1910.

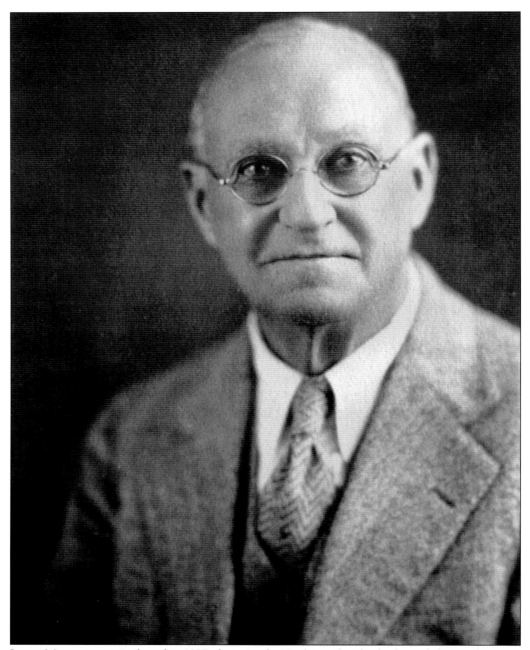

James Moore is pictured in this 1937 photograph. He, his wife, Elizabeth, and their young son, Otho, drove a team into the valley in 1898 and stayed for a while with Elizabeth Moore's brother at his homestead where the present Date Festival Grounds are located. The property was covered with mesquite trees, and the house was little more than a shack. Nevertheless, in 1899, James and his family came to settle permanently, arriving by train in an "Immigration Car." It was loaded with farming equipment at the Monrovia, California, siding and unloaded at the Indio siding, and included a well rig, several tons of hay, lumber, nails, rolls of wire, and a milk cow. This time, they had their own homestead.

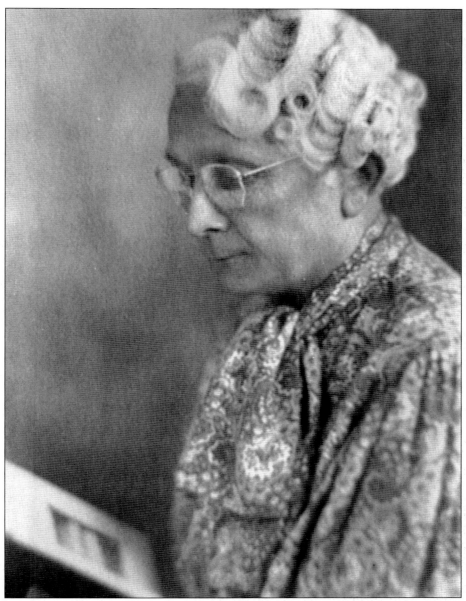

Elizabeth Moore, shown in this 1937 photograph, was characterized by her contemporaries and later residents as the "Pioneer Mother of Indio." In 1899, the family stayed with her brother, Lincoln Casebeer, until their own simple tent house was ready. It was the first of a number of small homes where the family lived in the early days. Elizabeth Moore said that the early homesteaders battled continuously against burros, coyotes, jackrabbits, and wild cattle. There was the noise of shotgun fire from every homestead. The rabbits were good for stew, but the burros were the greatest nuisances. Prospectors were plentiful, and they pastured their burros in Albert Tingman's corral, but they didn't stay pastured. Settlers barricaded their precious vegetable gardens with hay bales surrounded with barbed wire, but the animals got in anyway. Elizabeth Moore said, "The homestead was a noisy, dusty place until we drove those tramps out into the desert." She was one of the original members of the Altruain Literary Club, organized in 1912.

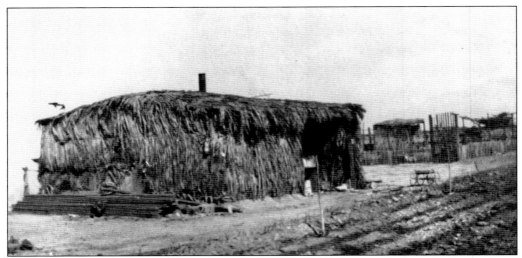

This palm-frond house on Fargo Street was the first home of Edith Mann Ross when the family arrived in 1896. It resembles many of the Native American homes. Edith remembered walking beside her family's wagon on the way from Vancouver, Washington, to the desert. They came seeking a warm, dry climate for Edith's mother.

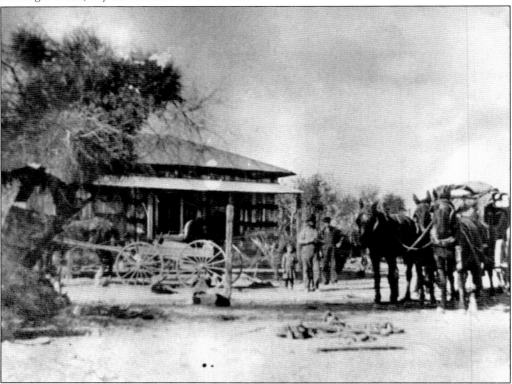

Edith's future husband, Bailey Ross, is shown in this photograph taken in front of his parents' home north of the railroad tracks. Note the double roof and wide porch. After her marriage, Edith was reported to have a beautifully appointed parlor with a Victor gramophone—the first mechanical music-maker in town.

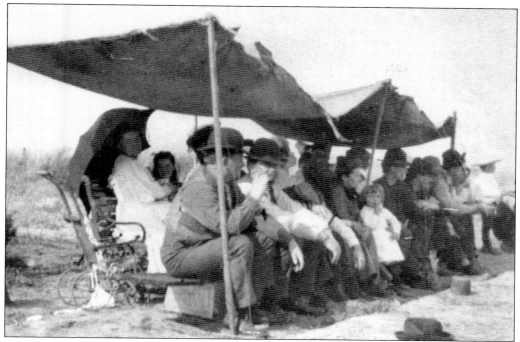

Life was not all work at the beginning of the 20th century. This crowd, under a makeshift shade structure, is enjoying a baseball game. The Coachella Valley was really one extended community in the early days. Quite likely, some of the spectators would have come by train from Coachella, Thermal, or Mecca if they knew of the game to be played in Indio. A 1915 Indio team is shown in the lower picture.

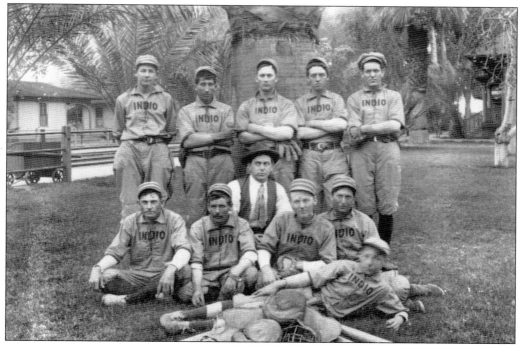

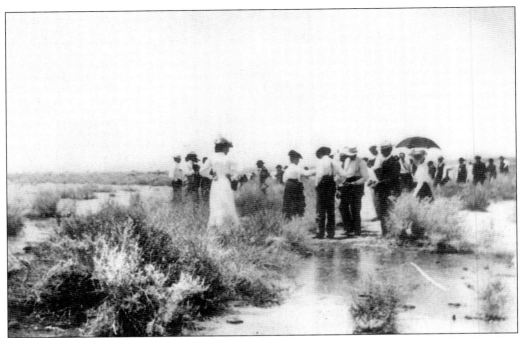

After 1906, the Southern Pacific Railroad offered excursions to the newly formed Salton Sea, 25 miles south of Indio. It was a popular picnic spot, and the railroad even provided sightseeing cruises out on the sea. Railroad tracks had to be moved to higher ground three times as the sea continued to rise, until the company managed to stop the flow of the Colorado River into the Salton Sink in 1907.

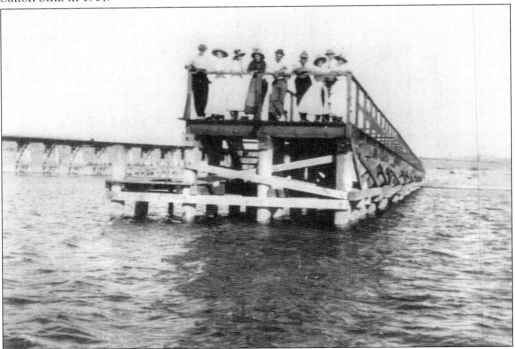

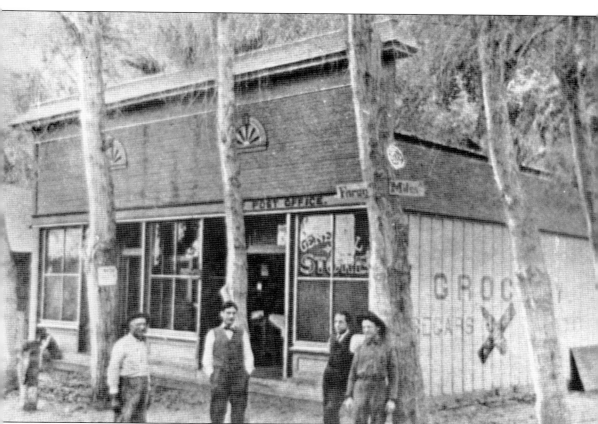

In 1906, Howard Ezra Gard became the owner of this more modern building that housed not only the grocery stock of the earlier Tingman store, but also general merchandise and the Indio Post Office. The store was near the corner of present-day Miles Avenue and Fargo Street, facing Fargo. Gard had come to the valley in the early 1900s and, until his tragic death in 1914, was active in both business and civic affairs. Just 24 years of age when he was appointed justice of the peace, he also owned an interest in the ice plant, the waterworks, and the remaining unsold lots in the town site. He also had the only livery rig in town—a team and buggy. Gard died as the result of burns suffered when gasoline from a leaking tank car on the railroad tracks accidentally ignited. Since there was no hospital in the valley, Gard was put on the train to Banning, where he died a week later.

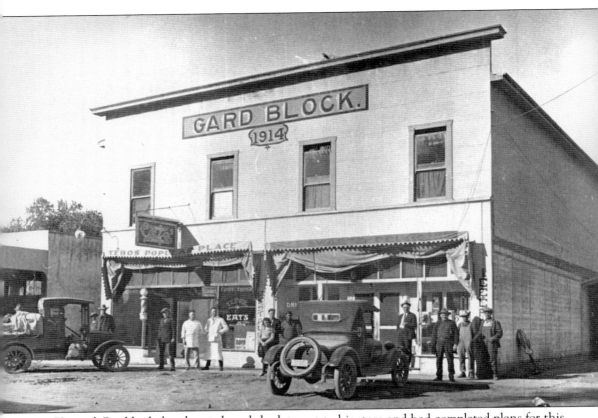

Howard Gard had already purchased the lot next to his store and had completed plans for this two-story, fire resistant building when he died in April 1914. His wife went ahead with the plans. They included space for two stores on the ground floor and a large lodge and dance hall above. Charles King was the real estate agent for the Southern Pacific Land Company, and he rented one of the new stores. The second store space was rented for a billiard parlor. Later Frank Tebo operated this billiard parlor and installed a lunch counter and a barber chair. Tebo also rented Gard Hall for Saturday night dances. Dr. Ralph Pawley remembered that his parents, who lived on a ranch near Coachella, would make a straw bed for their kids in the back of the farm wagon and drive to Indio for shopping and to attend the Saturday night dance at Gard Hall, arriving back at the ranch after sunrise on the following day.

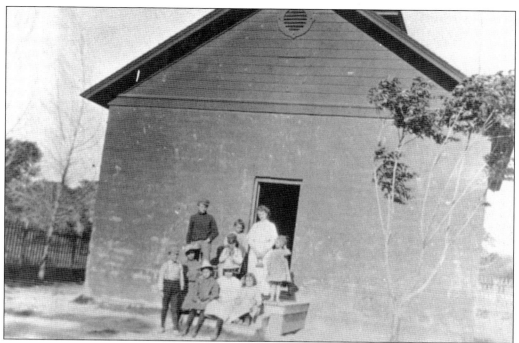

Since most of Indio's first residents were single men, there was no demand for a school until families began to arrive after 1896. The county superintendent of education required that there be at least seven students before the county would supply a teacher. Finally a family with four school-age children arrived, and a teacher was authorized. Classes were held in a tent until this adobe schoolhouse was finished. Before long, enrollment had doubled and then tripled.

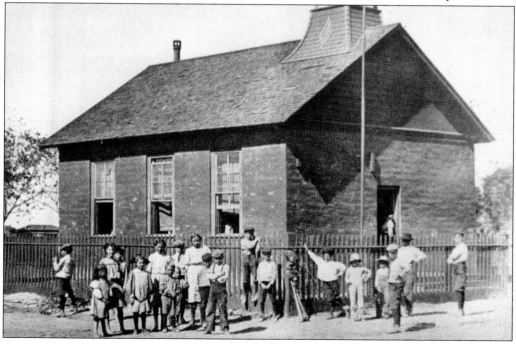

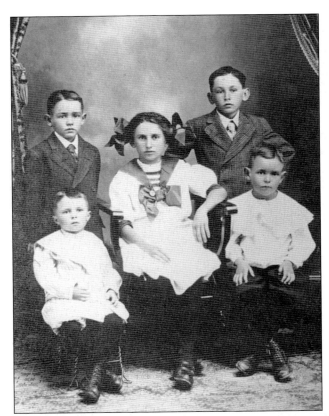

The school population was growing, as these 1912 photographs illustrate. In the left photograph, these children pose for a family portrait. They are, from left to right, (first row) Louis, Lucy, and Raymond; (second row) Leonard and Harlan. In the lower picture, Cinderella Courtney, the first white child born in the valley, is pictured on the steps of the Courtney home with a friend, David Elgin, and her sisters, Lucile and Viola.

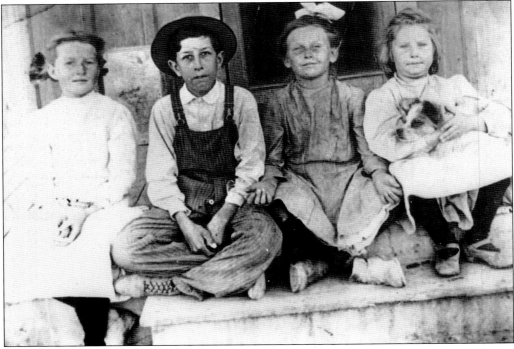

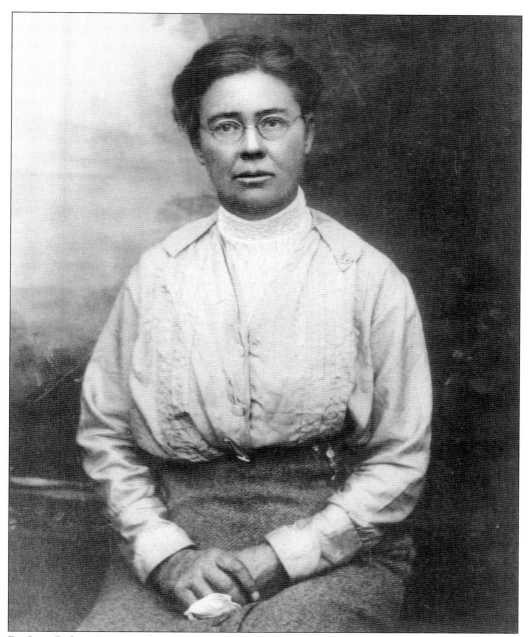

Dr. June Robertson arrived in Indio in 1904, intending to be "just a housewife," but she became the valley's first resident physician. Her husband had tuberculosis, and she accompanied him to the recommended warm, dry climate, leaving behind a medical practice in Nebraska. Her husband took over management of the Nelson Health Camp, and she became doctor to the tuberculosis patients, but she soon found herself called upon by the whole valley, from Palm Springs to the Salton Sea. Her specialty was delivering babies, but she also tended to all manner of emergencies, sending the most serious to the nearest hospital by train. She retired in 1916 when other doctors set up practice in the valley.

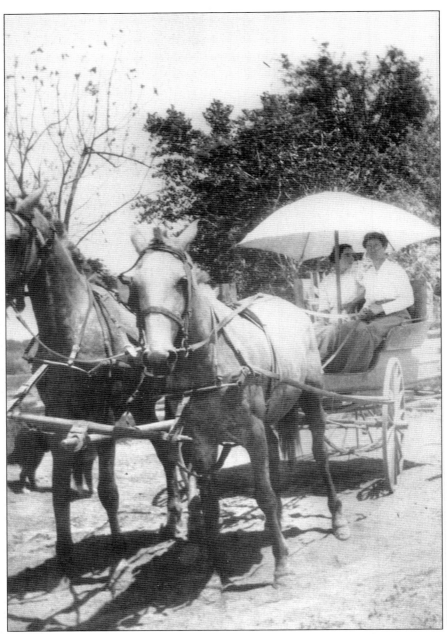

Dr. June Robertson was appointed by the Bureau of Indian Affairs to serve the Native American population. Many were distrustful of "white man's medicine," but she found an ally in Ambrosia, a native medicine man who recognized his limitations, especially in the face of a measles epidemic that decimated families. "Doc June," as she was called, traveled by horse-and-buggy at first, but getting through the sand to make house calls proved very difficult, and she soon simply traveled by horseback. It was reported that she carried a six-shooter, and few doubted that she could use it. Her husband died in 1914, and two years later, she married Frank McCarroll, the station agent in Indio. She became very involved in civic affairs after her retirement from the practice of medicine.

Typical of the women who helped settle the Coachella Valley was Margaret Brown McKay, pictured right in this 1890 photograph taken in Glasgow, Scotland. What a complete change awaited her in the California desert! In the lower photograph, she is shown on horseback with her children, Margaret and Henry, in 1910. She lost Henry shortly thereafter, the victim of an exploding kerosene stove in their home.

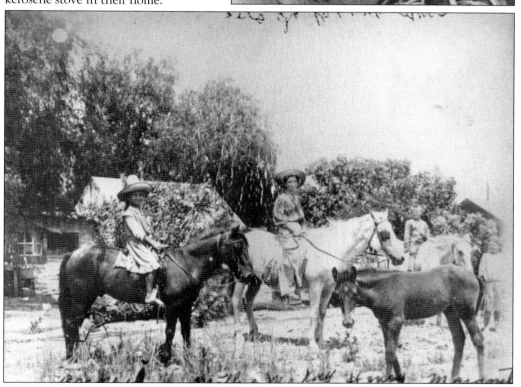

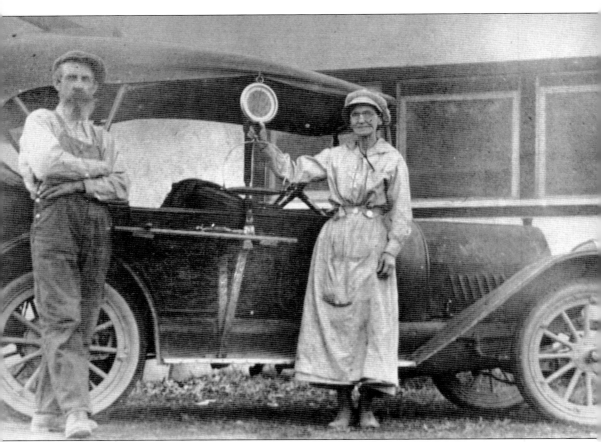

Margaret McKay and her husband, Henry, sold meat from this 1913 Chevrolet automobile. The arrival of automobiles in the valley greatly improved mobility, but the lack of paved roads made travel difficult. Note the scale hanging on the side of the car. Henry McKay had worked at the New Liverpool Salt Works before it was inundated by the new Salton Sea in 1905, and he sought other employment. He is credited with laying out the grid for valley roads and assigning them the numbers in use today. He named the north-south streets from Washington Street eastward for presidents of the United States in order of their presidency. These streets marked section lines, as did the east-west numbered streets.

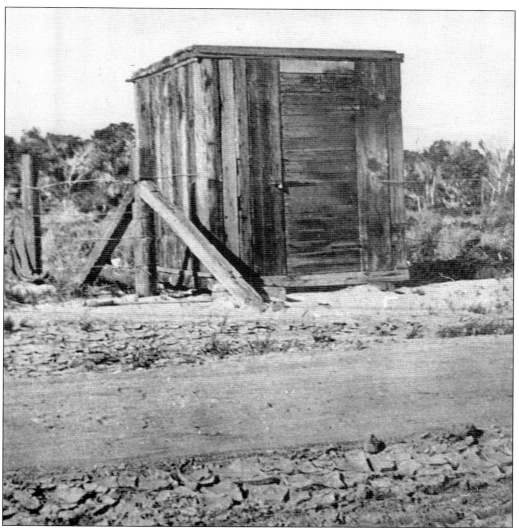
This earliest jail was replaced in 1909, but until then, it housed the town drunks or runaway boys (until their families picked them up) and an occasional bootlegger. When Riverside County was formed in 1893, the Riverside County Board of Supervisors declared the county to be "dry." This original jail was built of upended railroad ties, and there are conflicting accounts as to whether or not it had a roof. It was built by Johnny Boatwright, the town constable. The jail was located north of Miles Avenue and west of Smurr Street, not far from the railroad. Meals were prepared by a local café for the unfortunate soul confined there. Perhaps the primitive facility contributed to the fact that crime was rare. Note the caked mud in the foreground, indicating the recent passage of a flood.

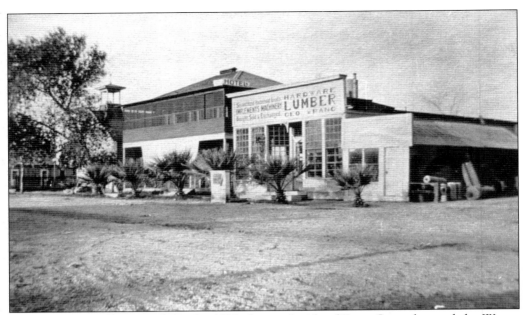

The street was still unpaved, but by 1915, the north side of Fargo Street boasted the Wrang Lumber Company and the Green Hotel among its businesses. Note the screened porch on the second story of the hotel.

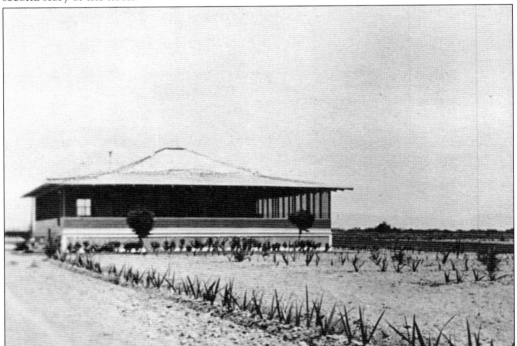

The home of Chester and Florence Sparey was built in 1915 on Jackson Street near Avenue 42. Its style reflected the desert architecture of a wide porch completely around the house, which protected the living areas from direct sunlight. Sparey was one of those far-sighted men who helped establish the Coachella Valley Water District in 1918.

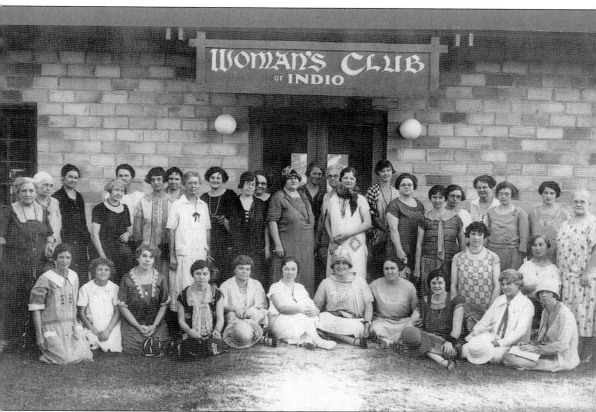

Dr. June Robertson McCarroll was a very active member of the Woman's Club of Indio, the successor to the Altruain Literary Club. As Indio grew, there were more and more "suitable" women wanting to join the club, and meeting in their homes limited the number of members they could invite to join. In this 1923 photograph, Dr. McCarroll is the woman in the white dress standing on the left side of the picture. The group is justly proud of their new clubhouse, which immediately became the locale of many civic and social gatherings. The clubhouse still stands at the corner of Miles Avenue and King Street—a location that was considered "way out of town" to many of the members who had to walk down the dusty, unpaved streets to get to meetings.

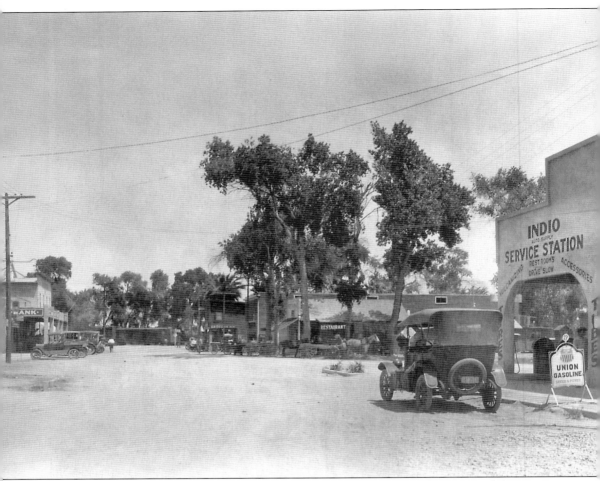

Fargo Street looked like this in 1913. Note the horse and wagon in the center of the picture. Automobiles were becoming more common in Indio in the 1920s, and "service stations" catered to locals and to the tourists passing through the valley on its poor roads. The Los Angeles–to–Phoenix Road Race came through Indio in 1908 and 1909. To help drivers stay on the route, local youths built bonfires at the turns in the road, staying up most of the night awaiting racers. When they heard the roar of engines, they would throw brush on the fire. An auto club publication stated that the worst stretch of road was that near Indio. A Buick won the race in 1909, requiring 19 hours and 40 minutes to complete the course.

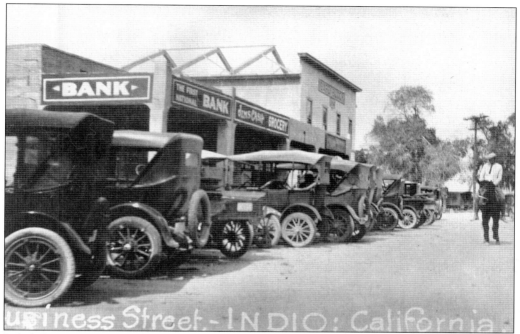

Labeled "Saturday afternoon street scene on Fargo Avenue," this 1925 collection of cars illustrates how Indio had grown. With increased automobile traffic, there were many more serious accidents. Dr. June Robertson McCarroll is credited with originating the idea of a painted line down the center of a roadway. Backed by the Woman's Club of Indio and the California Federation of Women's Clubs, she succeeded in getting the California Highway Department to try out the idea, and the rest is history. A section of I-10 freeway in the valley bears her name in recognition of her lifesaving idea.

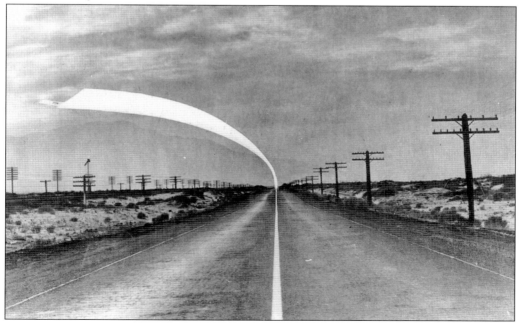

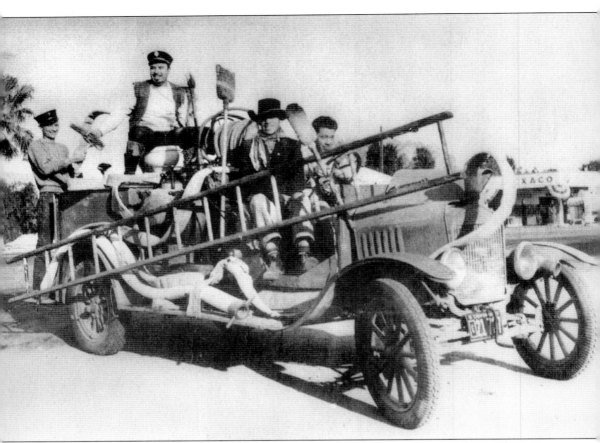

Indio's first fire truck arrived in 1924 amid much fanfare. Until that date, Indio residents were dependent on the Southern Pacific Railroad employees to battle fires. Their 1,000 feet of hose was laid across the tracks and highway, and if the fire was within reach of the hose, there was hope of saving the structure. Otherwise, it was the bucket brigade. A fire engine was of no value without a water system and fire hydrants, and that infrastructure had to be put in place by willing taxpayers. It was a struggle, led by the owner and publisher of the *Date Palm* newspaper. The fire department was an all-volunteer group of firefighters at first. The used engine cost $2,000 and bore the inscription, "Tiajuana FD." The fire truck made many parades in later years, as this 1930 photograph shows.

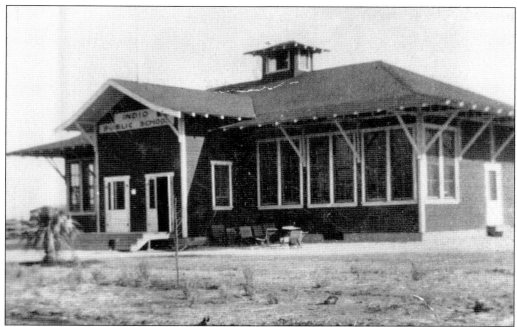

Indio outgrew the original adobe schoolhouse, and by 1909, this new, frame, two-room school had been built. It served students for many years and now has been moved to the grounds of the Coachella Valley Historical Society museum on Miles Avenue and renovated to depict a typical early school to museum visitors. The lower photograph shows students in front of Indio's third school, the Lincoln School. This was a four-room, red hollow-tile building constructed in 1926 on property next to the present Greyhound bus depot on Oasis Street.

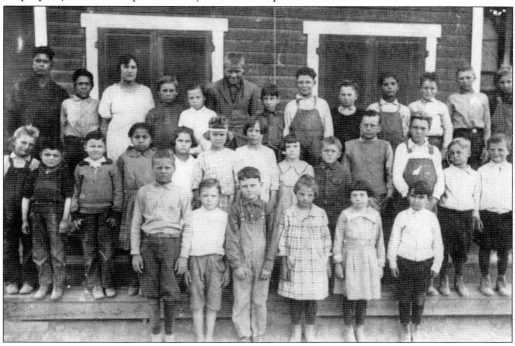

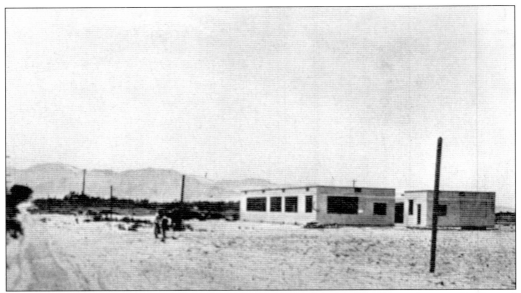

Indio students attended the valley's first (and only) high school built on Airport Boulevard in 1916. In 1911, the first classes were held in Thermal and then at a site in Coachella. The Airport Boulevard site was donated to the Coachella Valley Joint Union School District and was approximately equidistant from the three main valley towns—Indio, Coachella, and Thermal. Each town wanted the school to be built there, and the compromise pleased no one, but the school board prevailed. One argument in favor of the rural site was that it kept the students away from the bad influence of the towns' pool halls. The lower photograph, taken about 1939, shows the expanded campus that served all of the Coachella Valley except the Palm Springs area. That area's residents opened their own high school that year, ending a commute to Banning for their high school students.

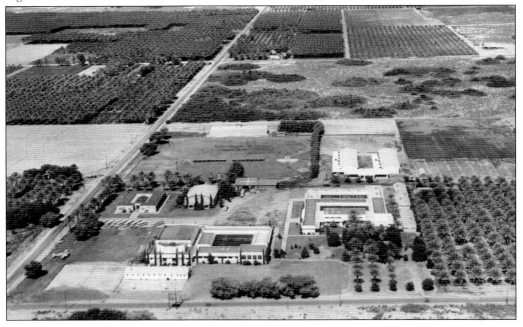

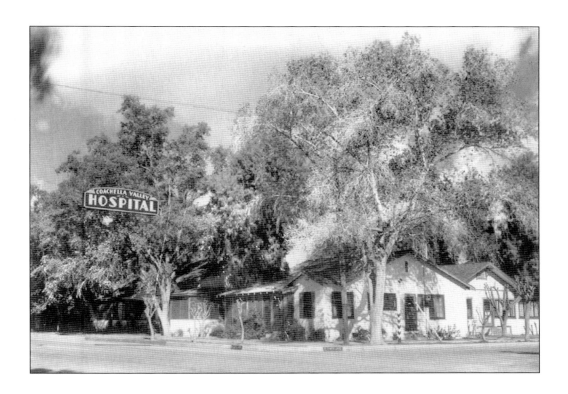

The valley's first hospital is pictured in the top photograph. It consisted of several small homes that were joined together and remodeled to provide treatment rooms and several beds. Dr. Russell Gray was in charge, and his wife served as nurse and cook. It was located at the northeast corner of Towne and Miles Avenues and opened in 1928. Casita Hospital opened in the late 1940s as Indio's second hospital. It was built by Dr. B. Gene Morris on the western edge of the city on Miles Avenue. It is obvious in this picture that Miles Avenue was not paved that far out of town.

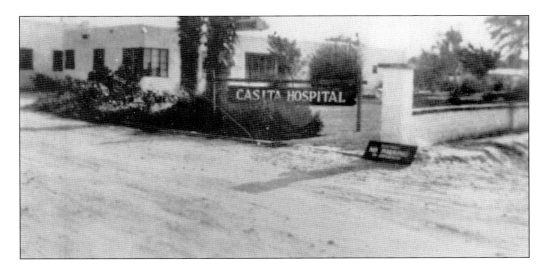

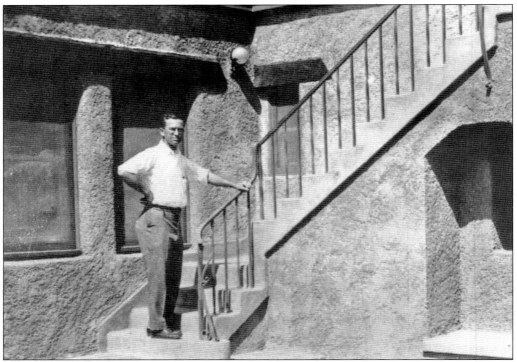

Dr. Harry Smiley and his wife, Nell, arrived in the valley in the early 1920s en route to Los Angeles to establish a medical practice. Their car broke down in Indio, and while it was being repaired, they took note of the fact that the town had no resident doctor. They decided to stay, renting rooms on Miles Avenue near Fargo Street for their first residence and office. In 1926, they built an adobe home/office that was called the finest structure in Indio at the time. Today it is the home of the Coachella Valley Museum and Cultural Center and is a fine example of adobe architecture of the period.

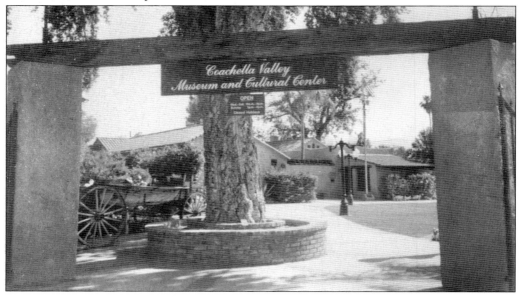

Dr. Reynaldo Carreon, a noted Los Angeles ophthalmologist, owned a home and land in Indio, and made regular trips to the desert to provide eye care for hundreds of local residents. Carreon had a passion for helping Hispanic students receive the higher education that was responsible for his own success in life. The Indio Community Hospital, located at the intersection of Monroe Street and Doctor Carreon Boulevard, was built on land originally owned by Dr. Carreon. The hospital became the John F. Kennedy Memorial Hospital in 1984. (Courtesy of the Dr. Reynaldo Carreon Foundation.)

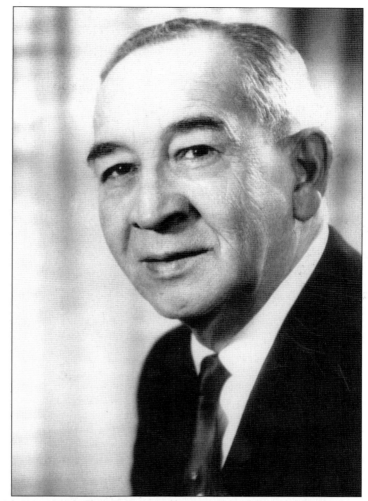

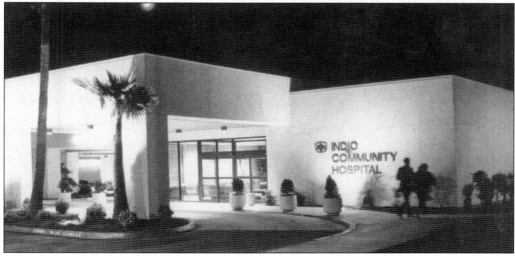

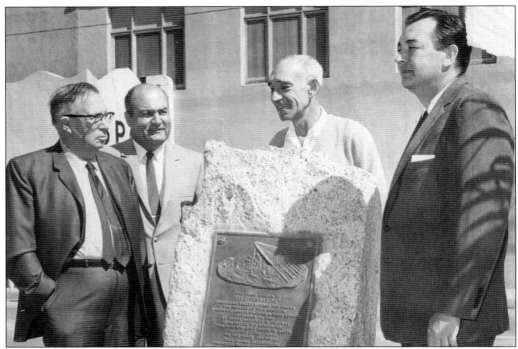

Pictured from left to right, Otho Moore, John Peters, Joe Patterson, and Tom Overhulse participated in the dedication of the plaque marking the site of the first newspaper published in the Coachella Valley on November 21, 1901. The marker is located on Bliss Street near the corner of Fargo Street in almost the exact site of that first printing office. The editor and publisher, Randolph Freeman, named the paper the *Submarine*, and he printed it himself on an old Michle Snapper hand press. A copy of the first edition is in the archives of the Coachella Valley Museum and Cultural Center. Good communication is essential to the growth of any enterprise, especially a town, and subsequent newspapers helped Indio become the first valley city to become incorporated.

THE SUBMARINE

Published weekly at Indio, Riverside County, California,— 22 feet below sea-level,—by RANDOLPH R. FREEMAN

Subscription, - $1.50 a year.

ADVERTISING, $1 50 per inch per month.

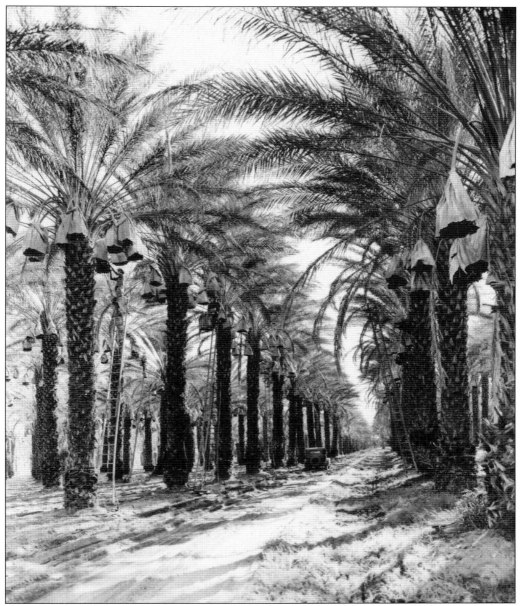

Indio's most enduring early newspaper was named the *Date Palm*. Its masthead proclaimed "Indio, California, Where Dates Grow." It was front-page news when new plantings of palms were made and the city was surrounded by beautiful palm groves like in this 25-year-old planting. When the U.S. Department of Agriculture located its date and citrus experiment station in Indio in 1907, Indio became the world center of date research. The first station was located near Mecca, but the rising Salton Sea threatened to flood it, so the work was transferred to land in Indio.

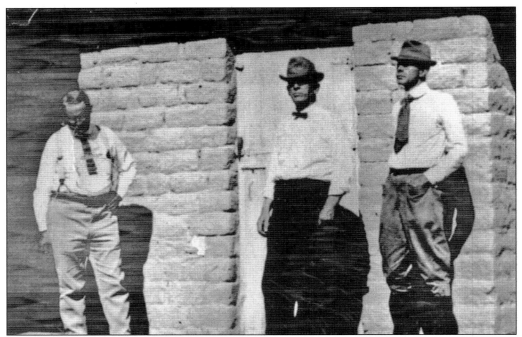

These three men—from left to right, Silas Mason, Frank Thackery, and Dr. Walter Swingle—were largely responsible for the acquisition and nurturing of leading Old World date varieties planted in the Coachella Valley from 1900 to 1927. Planting date seeds was not a viable way to establish a commercial date garden, so both Mason and Swingle made trips to North Africa and Egypt to arrange for importations of the date offshoots. Thackery worked at the U.S. Department of Agriculture date and citrus station in Indio, shown below.

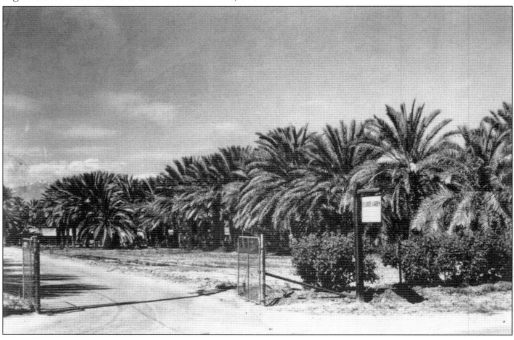

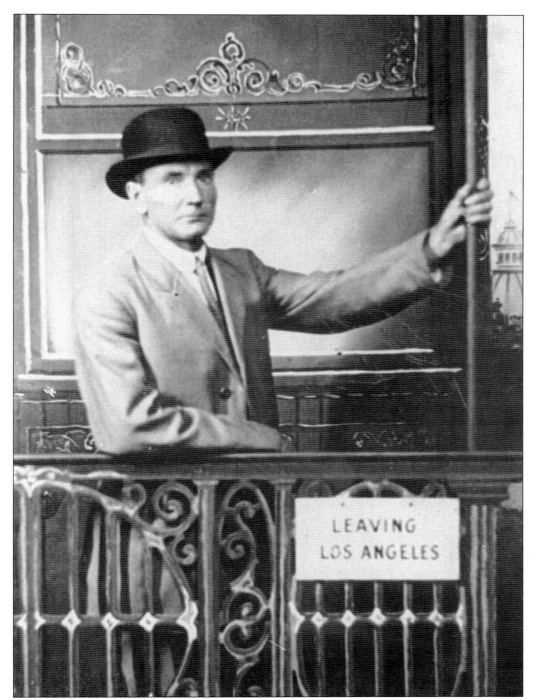

Bruce Drummond was the first superintendent of the government date garden in Indio. He served from 1907 to 1923. He quite literally developed the experiment station from bare land to a research facility that attracted scientists and date growers from all over the world. His daughter, Laura Drummond Pratt, furnished many of the very early photographs of Indio.

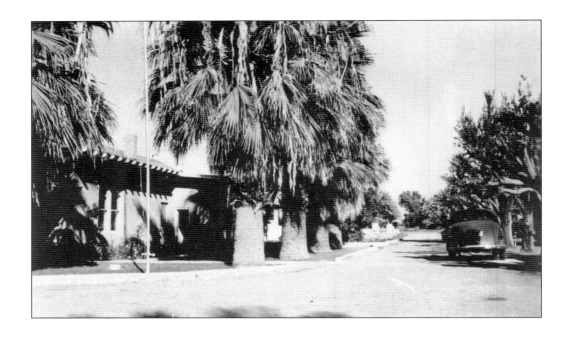

Two views show the buildings at the government date garden. It was located on Clinton Street, west of Indio at the time of its establishment in 1907. Over the years, the city grew west to surround the property. Budget cuts in the early 1980s forced the garden's closure, and a housing development occupies the site now.

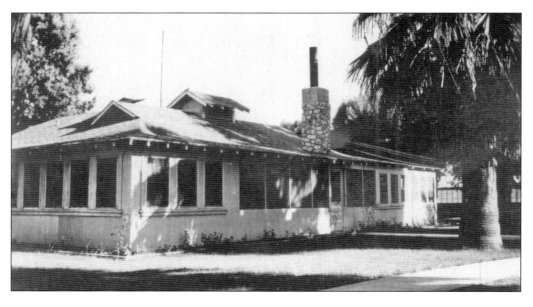

Roy Nixon brought international fame to Indio as the horticulturist in charge of date research at the U.S. Department of Agriculture station. Date growing was an ancient practice in North Africa and the Middle East, but very little had been done to improve cultural practices over the years. The work of the Indio station was shared with local growers and with visitors from the Old World. Nixon made several trips abroad, one on a Guggenheim scholarship, to learn more and to share his own research. He was a good-will ambassador to those countries he visited.

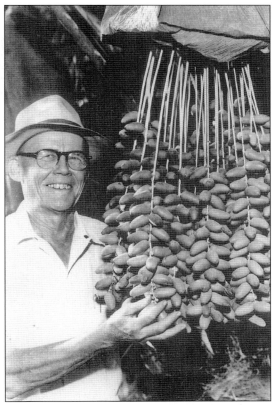

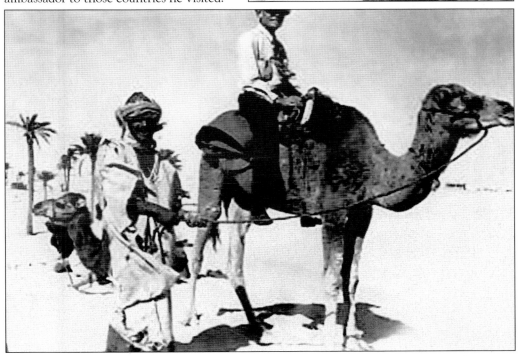

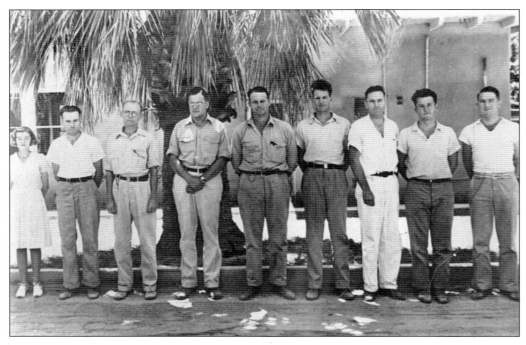

Roy Nixon is pictured third from the left in this photograph of the staff at the U.S. Department of Agriculture station. Employees worked with farmers to solve problems related to this new agricultural industry. In the lower picture, children of station employees cool off in a watering tank that made a great swimming pool. Pictured from left to right are Stewart Nixon, Margaret Moore, and Jean Berger in the summer of 1937.

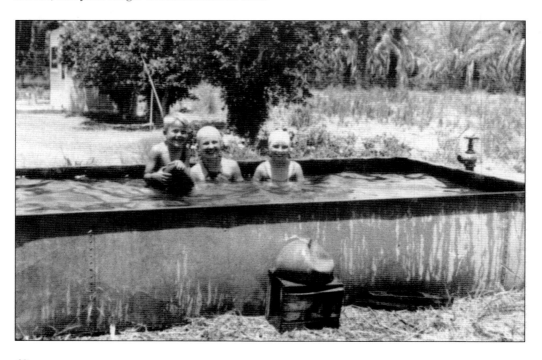

There was still a great deal of desert land surrounding the valley's date gardens, and rattlesnakes were a common hazard. In this photograph, Caleb Cook, for whom Cook Street is named, displays one caught on his date garden west of Indio. Re-leveling and putting in borders on the Cook ranch was done with this three-mule team and a Fresno scraper in 1936.

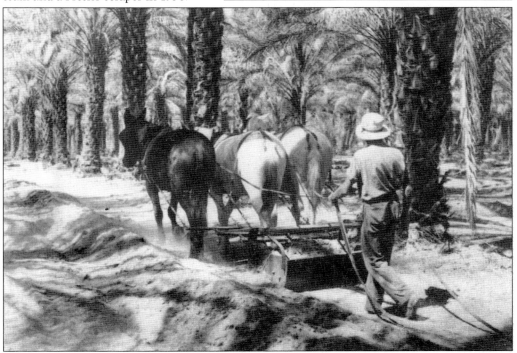

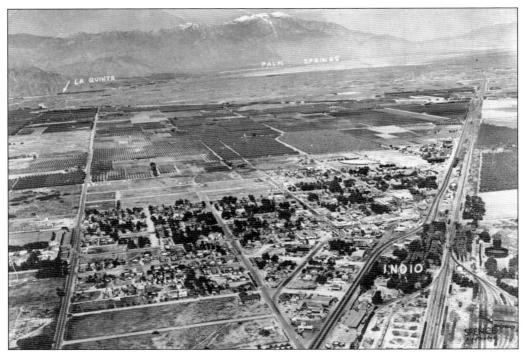

In this 1938 photograph of Indio, the railroad and Highway 99 are in the foreground, the town in the center, and a wide expanse of date gardens and vineyards looks toward Palm Springs in the back. Indio was truly the "hub of the valley" in the 1930s. The lower photograph shows a close-up of one of the beautiful producing date gardens visible in the top picture.

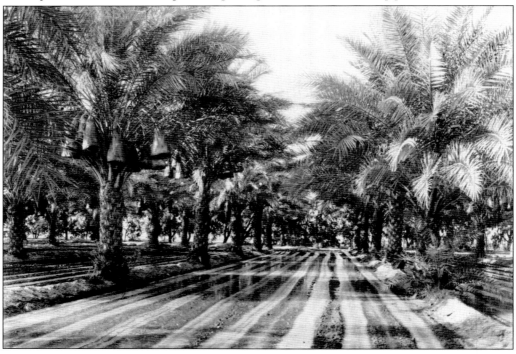

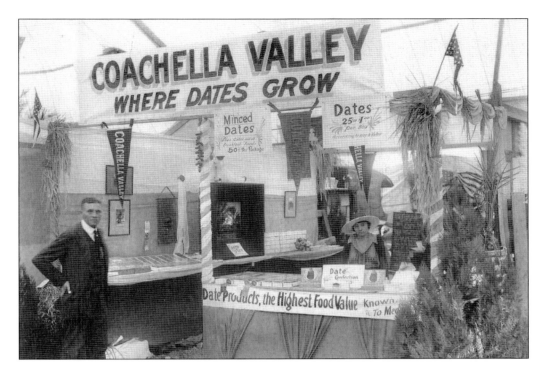

Indio began to advertise its dates with this display at the Riverside County Fair in Riverside in 1915. Dates were truly an exotic crop, and their production here in the desert attracted many interested farmers and even absentee landowners. In the lower picture, one of the showplaces near Indio was the Sniff Date Garden, just west of Indio on Highway 111. Dr. Sniff planted subtropical plants under his palms, creating a beautiful tourist attraction.

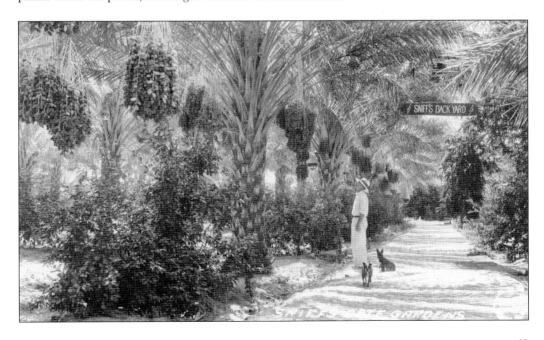

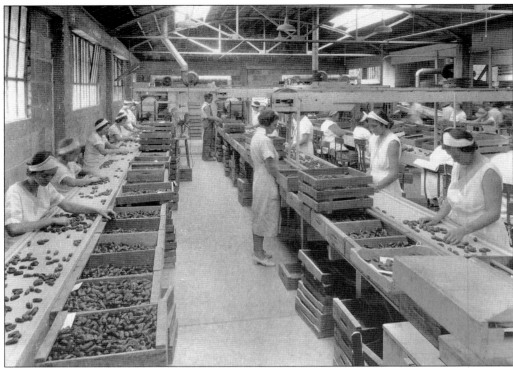

The first date-packing cooperative started in Indio in 1919. Total production of dates had grown to the point that uniform grading and marketing was essential. This view of the Deglet Noor Date Growers packing plant shows how far this new agricultural enterprise had come in less than 20 years. Most of these dates were destined for the wholesale market. Small growers of date varieties other than Deglet Noor frequently sold their dates to the many retail shops, like the Ripple Date Shop pictured below.

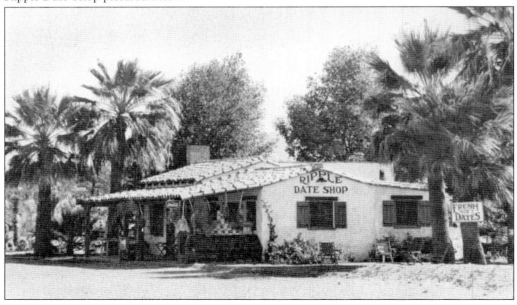

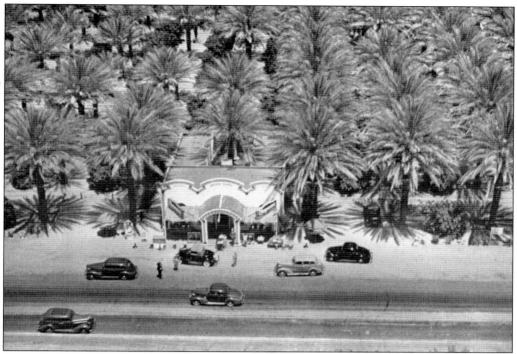

Two views show the Sun Gold Date Shop and Date Garden located on Highway 111 just west of Indio. Taken in 1937, the top photograph shows the beautiful symmetrical rows of palms reminiscent of the columns in ancient temples. In fact, historians believe that the date palm was the inspiration for those early buildings. The fancy car in the lower photograph, taken in 1938, suggests the wealthy clientele who were intrigued by this exotic crop. This date garden and shop were later owned by the Codekas family. The land is now part of the city of Indio and is being developed into a modern shopping and residential center.

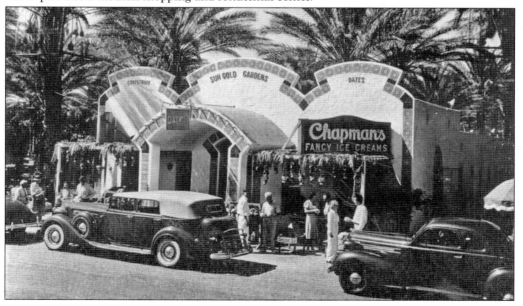

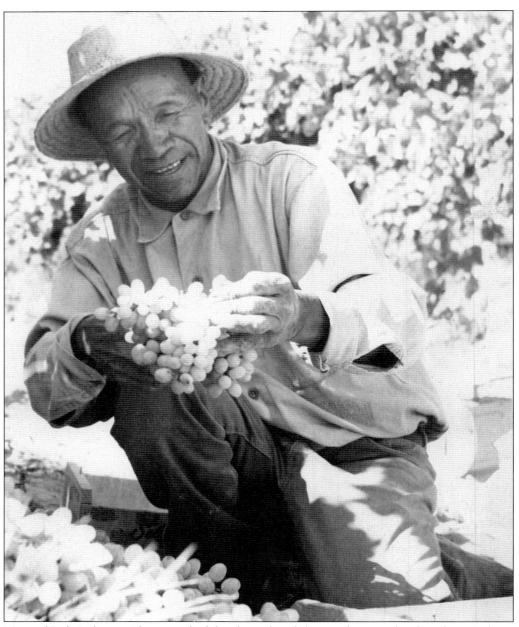

Most of Indio's first residents worked for the railroad, but as the area developed, agriculture assumed a larger role in the business of the city. When it was discovered that grapes ripened in the Coachella Valley weeks ahead of other areas, giving local growers the advantage of higher early market prices, acres of vineyards ringed the city. The railroad provided refrigerated cars to enable shippers to send the fruit to distant markets.

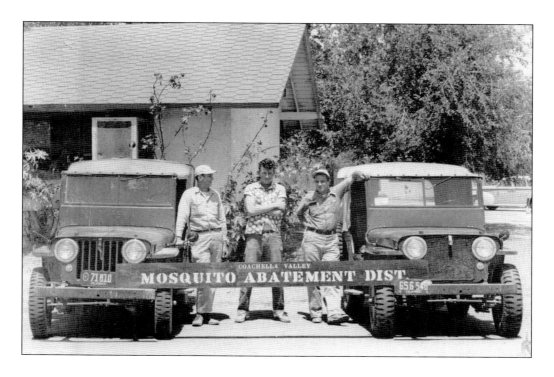

As more land came under cultivation, two extremely annoying pests threatened to put a halt to population growth. Eye gnats and mosquitoes flourished in the damp, cultivated soil, and the valley pleaded for the creation of a district to control the problem. The Indio Women's Club led the fight, and in 1928, two years before Indio's incorporation, the Coachella Valley Mosquito Abatement District received its charter. Palm Springs resisted being part of the district, having little farmland near it and less of a problem, but eventually, all of the valley cities followed Indio's lead.

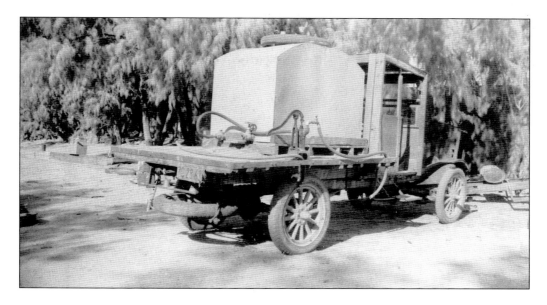

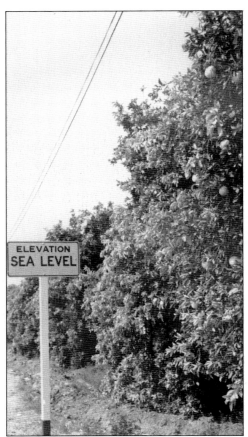

This sign on Highway 99 (now Indio Boulevard) stood near the northern city limits for many years, a reminder that most of the city was below sea level. Coachella Valley grapefruit was soon world famous, and there were many groves within and surrounding Indio. The fan palms in the lower photograph were known as "sea level palms" since they were located near the sea level sign. They also marked one of the early showplaces of Indio—the Durbrow Ranch. It was considered "way out of town" in the early 1900s.

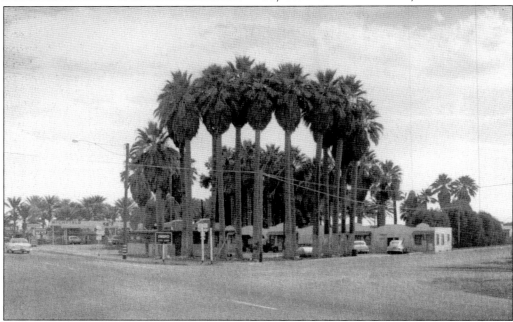

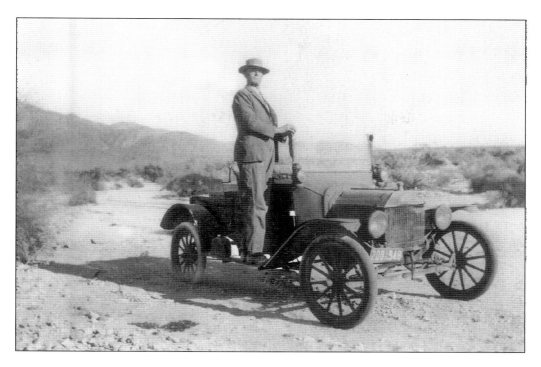

Indio's streets remained unpaved for many years, but they were much improved over the roads leading into the valley. Travelers from the east entered the valley through Box Canyon. The top photograph shows Indio merchant Charles Green "on the road to Blythe" in 1923. The lower photograph, taken by Otho Moore in 1920, shows the Box Canyon road.

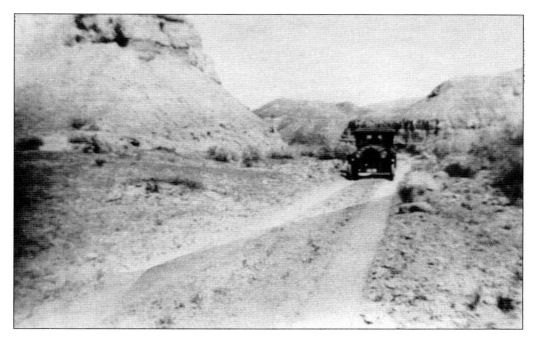

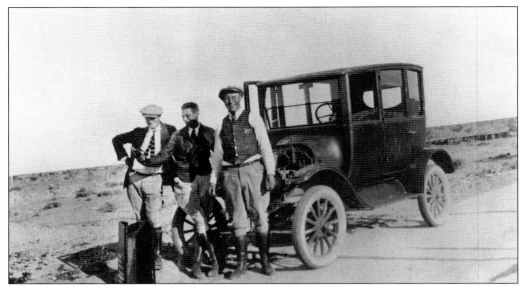

There was a big push to pave the road from Indio to Palm Springs, and this photograph shows a stretch of completed concrete roadway. Cars were quite unreliable, however, and the caption on the top picture says, "Should have known better!" There was a real celebration when Highway 99 from Edom (Thousand Palms) to Indio was finally paved in 1927. The small sign in the right of the lower picture advises travelers to go via Palm Springs during a sandstorm. Blowing sand on that section of Highway 99 was a problem for many years. Indio citizens and particularly the newspaper promoted highway improvements, which were key to the city's growth.

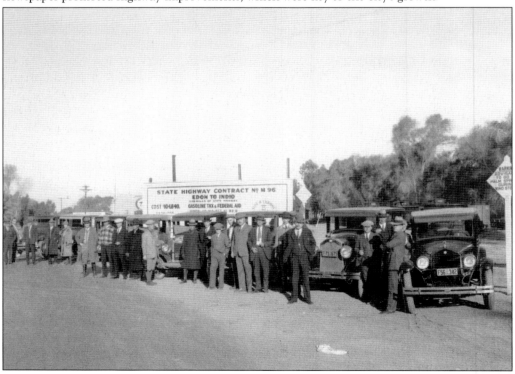

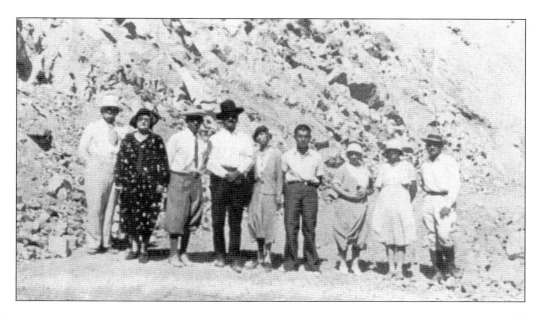

In 1932, the first road into the western mountains was completed from Highway 111 in what is now Palm Desert to Pinyon Crest in the Santa Rosa Mountains. It was quite an amazing engineering feat. Known as the "palms to pines" highway, it enabled valley residents to reach the cool mountain areas without going first to Banning and taking a road up the gentler western slope. J. Win Wilson (in the white suit on the left) and his wife, Josephine (standing next to him), joined other leading citizens in celebrating the opening of the road. Wilson was the editor of the *Date Palm* newspaper, which had led the campaign for the road. In the lower photograph, pioneers picnic on the road to Cottonwood Springs.

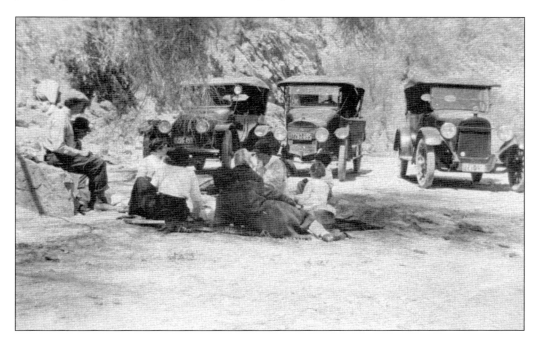

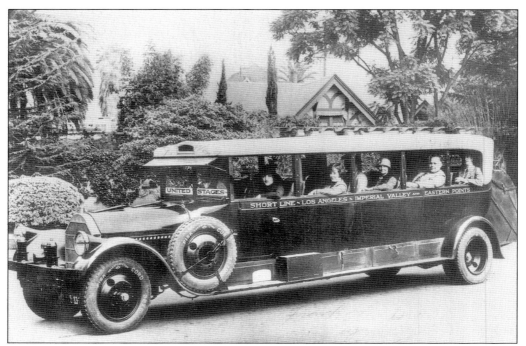

In 1924, there was regular bus service to and through Indio. The lower photograph shows how narrow the concrete road was and how soft the sandy edge appeared. Besides being narrow, the roadway was almost the same color as the sand, and there were many accidents, as a wheel would slip off the edge and cause the car to overturn. Dr. June Robertson McCarroll conceived the idea of painting a line down the narrow roadway to help drivers stay on their half of the road, and with the support of the Indio Woman's Club and the California Federation of Women's Clubs, her idea was adopted by the California Highway Department in 1927.

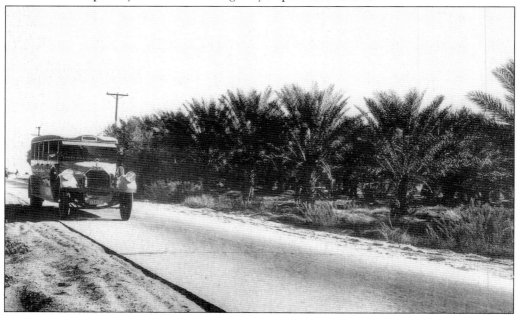

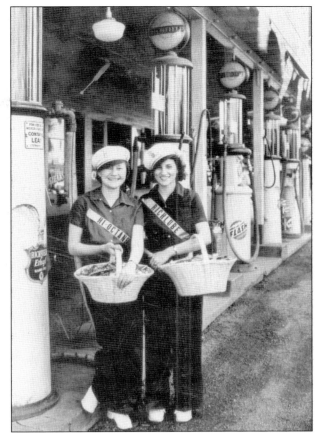

As automobile traveling became popular in the 1920s and 1930s, Indio was a logical stopping place on travels east and west across the desert. Service stations and auto camps were plentiful. In the right photograph, Lucille Tune Cavanaugh (left) and Joyce Pearson Reddish dispense smiles and local dates to travelers stopping at "Mac" McCausland's Richfield station. In the lower photograph, the sign advertises vulcanizing, a reminder of the days when recapping tires was common practice and the hot desert roads were hard on tires. Pictured is Art Woods's Texaco station. Almost every major oil company had a service station in Indio.

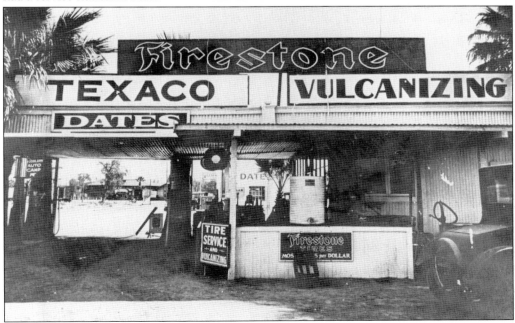

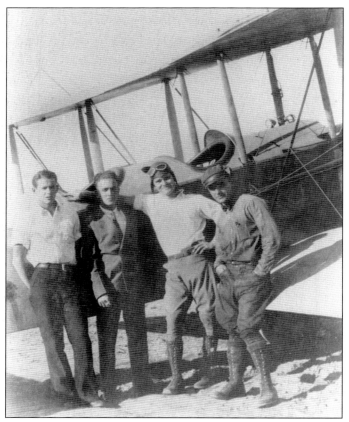

The automobile brought people to and through Indio, but so did the early airplanes. Members of the local flying club are shown in the left photograph, taken in 1927. Indio's first airport was located south of the city on property bordering Highway 99. The early airports were called "air fields" because that is what they were—just cleared fields on which planes could land and take off. Ray Thomas (left) and Sig Varian pose beside their plane in the lower photograph at the same location. Commercial flights were made into Indio by American Airlines, which had an office at the field, and there was airmail delivery to Indio. Sig Varian is one of the co-inventors of the Klystron tube, considered the basis for today's microwave technology.

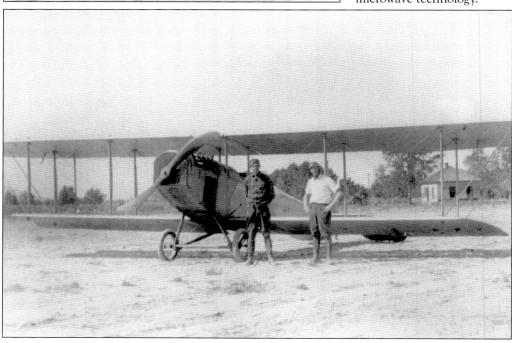

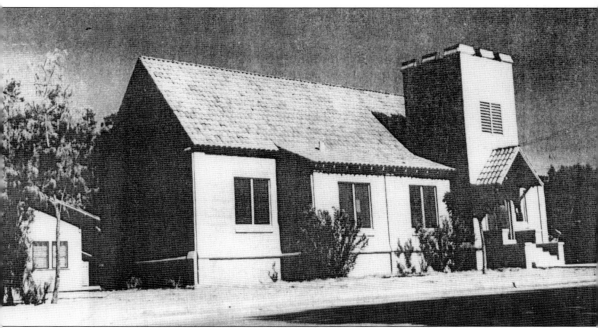

In 1909, the Indio Methodist Church was organized with 22 members. Various churches met in the school or other meeting rooms, but this building was probably the first permanent church building in Indio. The congregation sold their first building to the Odd Fellows Lodge, and in 1920, the congregation purchased a lot at the corner of Requa and Jackson Streets and constructed this building, which was used by the church until their move to the new facility on Requa and Deglet Noor Streets. The building was purchased by the Fitzhenry family for use as a chapel and mortuary. In 1937, Our Lady of Perpetual Help Catholic Church was established in Indio, and other denominations followed.

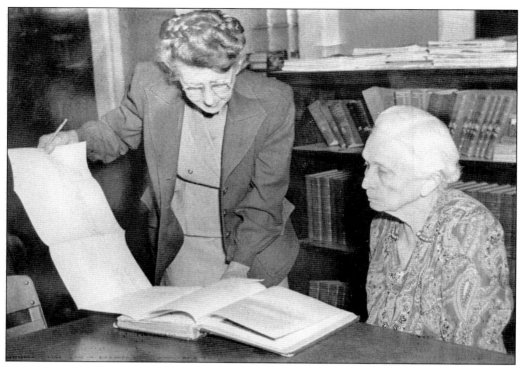

No story of creating the community would be complete without reference to Indio's growth in culture. In the top photograph, city librarian Jane Walker (left) and pioneer resident Elizabeth Moore look over an 1863 railroad survey book. Indio's first collection of library books was maintained by the Indio Woman's Club, but a permanent library building was erected on the northwest corner of Miles Avenue and Deglet Noor Street. In 2007, the building was leased to the Coachella Valley Historical Society to use as a date history museum. The Indio Library has moved to larger quarters. In the lower photograph, several early residents enjoy music in Box Canyon thanks to the gramophone and records they took with them on an outing.

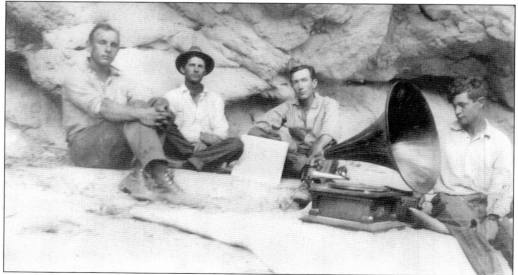

Four

INDIO WAS A MINING TOWN

From their earliest days, Indio and Mecca were the provisioning spots for prospectors searching for gold in the mountains surrounding the Coachella Valley. Albert Tingman, the station agent in Indio, recognized the business potential in serving the prospectors as they prepared to go "into the hills." Apparently Tingman grubstaked many of the miners. There is no record of just how much gold was taken out of the eastern mountains, but one report put the amount at $62 million. The mines were rich enough that Tingman sold his store and went into mining full time. The photograph shows Tingman's corral in 1900, located near present-day Miles Avenue and Fargo Street. Note the large sand dune in the background. There was a ravine in front of the store, and Tingman constructed a bridge so that people could get across to the railroad station.

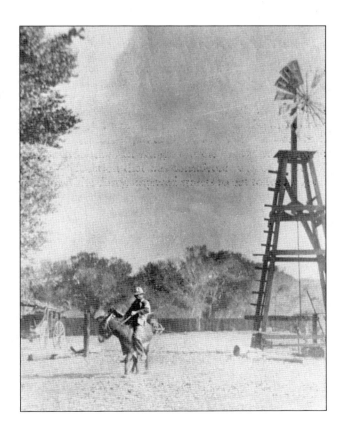

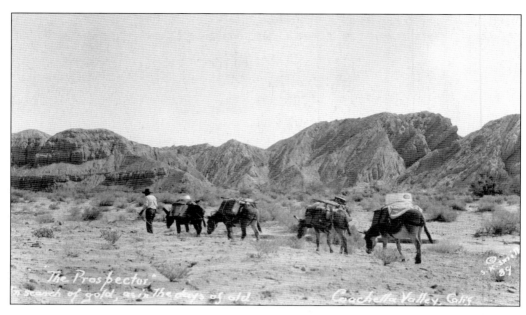

Before the discovery of adequate water for agriculture, the excitement in Coachella Valley was gold. Some prospectors simply headed into the hills with a string of mules, as shown in the top photograph. The dry hills east of Indio looked quite daunting, but there were a number of mines along the trail up to the Pinto Basin diggings. In the lower photograph, miners in the Hurkey Creek area of Mount San Jacinto take a break. This photograph was made about 1920 by Otho Moore, so mining was still attracting attention at that time.

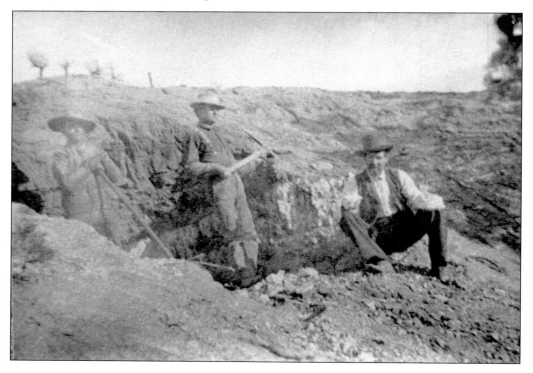

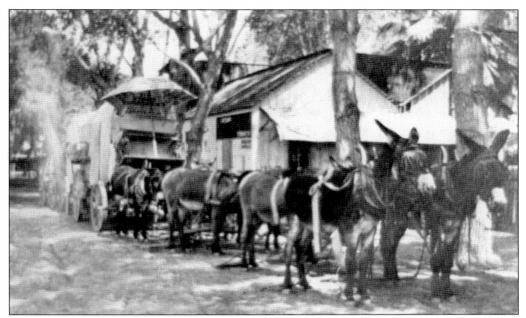

In the 1909 photograph above, an eight-mule freighting team loads up behind the Tallent Store. No men were more in demand than the experienced teamsters with their heavy wagons and sturdy mules and horses. Mines had to be supplied and gold and silver brought out of the mountains to the railroad. The Blue Cut Road was a teamster's highway. After loading their wagons at the Indio Freight Depot, they followed a sandy trail along the present route of Dillon Road, then they turned up Berdoo Canyon to the mining areas. The lower photograph is labeled "Freighting to Dale Mining District 1901."

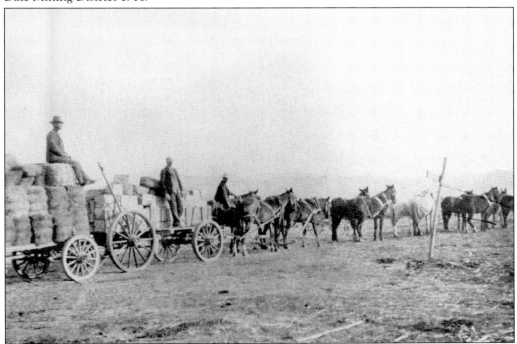

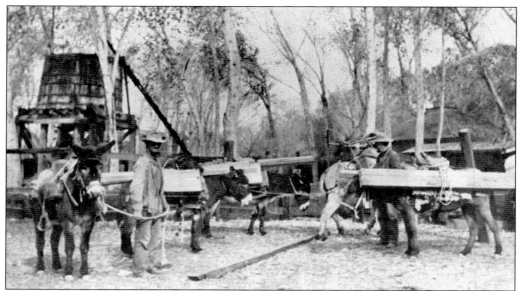

The Blue Cut Road supplied all of the mines in the present location of Joshua Tree National Park. According to Paul Wilhelm, naturalist and valley historian, there were more than 1,000 mines, shafts, and tunnels in the Pinto Mountains and in Gold Park, north of Pinto Basin. Efforts by the miners to have their claims excluded from the national monument when it was first created went on for years, but the federal government managed to gain control of most of the disputed land. These two pictures, both made around 1901, depict preparations for a trip. Museum archives record some dispute as to whether the lower picture shows a settler's wagons or a mining teamster's outfit. Both activities were going on in the early 1900s.

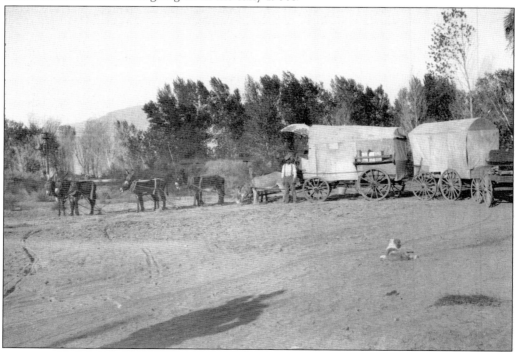

10,000 PEOPLE IN INDIO

in the Next Six Years is the prediction of a well known disinterested man in another community

This will happen provided we make our community attractive to these people coming in to work on the Aqueduct. We are doing our part by letting the world know the attractions here. Do your part by your own acts and words, and Subscribe to a copy of this paper for someone contemplating locating here. The cost of Two Dollars would not pay postage on the quantity of up-to-date information that can be sent this way each week for a year.

On May 26, 1930, the citizens of Indio voted to incorporate, making it the first incorporated city in the Coachella Valley. The Depression hit the valley hard, but Indio experienced a resurgence of mining activity in the 1930s that made those tough times much better than in other parts of the country. The Metropolitan Water District of Southern California was organized in 1928 by a group of far-sighted men whose aim was to plan, build, and pay for the huge Colorado River Aqueduct. It would deliver supplementary water to the thirsty coastal plain, and it would require 92 miles of tunnels, most of which would pass through the mountains east and north of Indio. Miners, experienced and inexperienced, flocked to Indio looking for work.

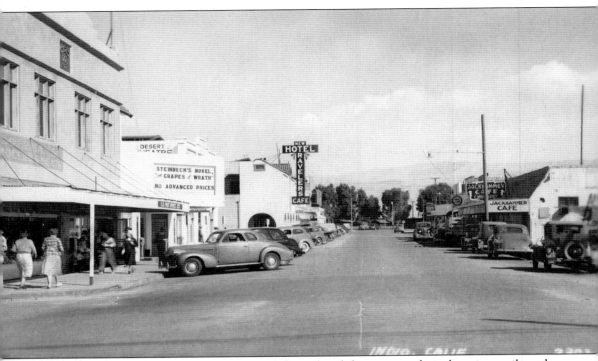

Fargo Street in the 1930s, looking toward the railroad depot, was relatively quiet until payday occurred at the aqueduct camps. The tunneling was done in sections, and there were eight camps immediately east of Indio—Yellow Canyon, Fargo, Berdoo, Pushawalla, 1,000 Palms, East Wide, Long Canyon, and Little Morongo. On payday, crew bosses and local merchants provided transportation to Indio and Coachella. Indio took on the appearance of a Wild West town at times. There was fierce competition between the various crews, hard-rock mining contests were well advertised, and hotels and motels were filled. One drilling contest drew more than 50 two-man teams representing every tunnel job on the project. The winners of a $500 prize drilled a hole five and a half feet through a huge granite boulder in 5 minutes and 38 seconds.

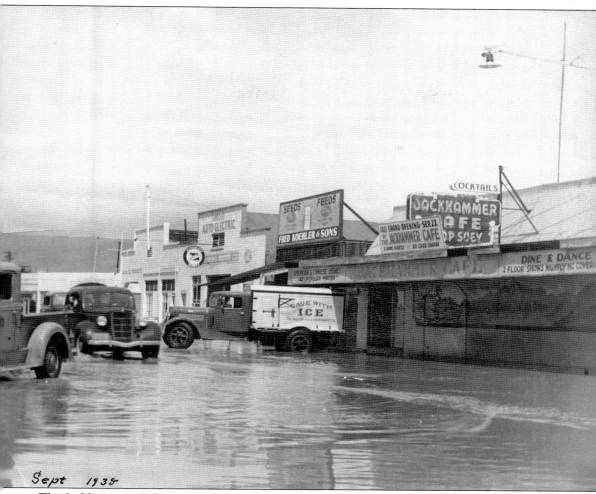

Sept 1938

The Jackhammer Café was one of Indio's most famous (and infamous) establishments during the 1930s. They advertised their Chinese and American menu and also claimed to be the most popular nightclub in the desert. A newspaper advertisement stated, "Private parties are invited and an orderly house is guaranteed." Apparently the latter was hard to guarantee when the miners descended on it, and many locals avoided Fargo Street at those times. However, there was little violent crime, and disorderly conduct was the main charge that put miners in jail. Crew bosses came on Monday morning to pick up any stragglers. Jobs were scarce, and even a $5-a-day job at hard labor was appreciated.

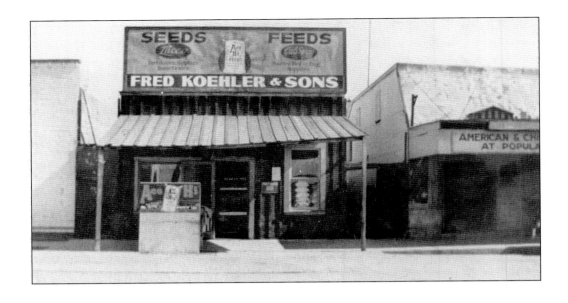

Koehler's Seed and Feed store was located next to the Jackhammer. They owned Indio's first business license. This building, on Fargo Street, was built about 1924. The family came to the valley in 1909. The interior of the store is shown in the lower photograph.

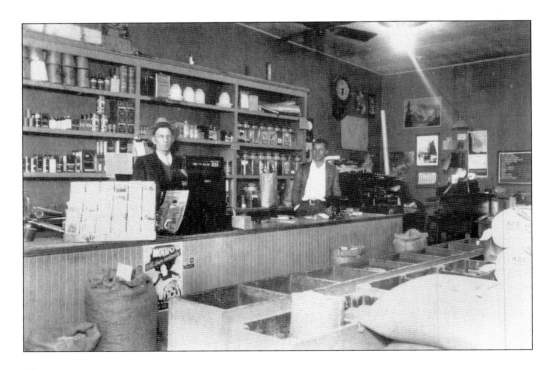

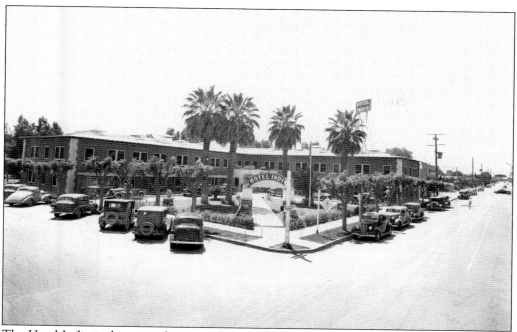

The Hotel Indio is shown in this 1935 photograph above. The aqueduct project was very good for business. The *Date Palm* of July 28, 1933, reported that the Potter Hotel was going to close for the summer, but "aqueduct activities have induced the Travelers' Hotel and the Hotel Indio to install cooling systems and to remain open for that clientele. Several eating places that formerly depended on tourist trade and normally closed have decided to remain open this summer to care for aqueduct workers patronage." Predictably, the Jackhammer was open year-round!

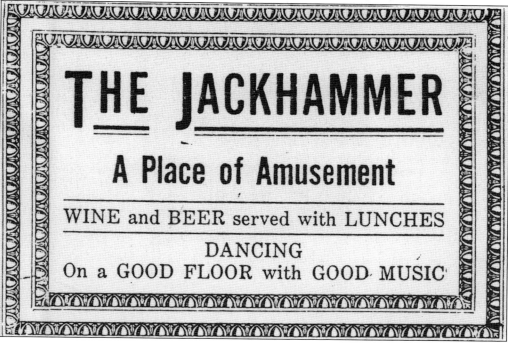

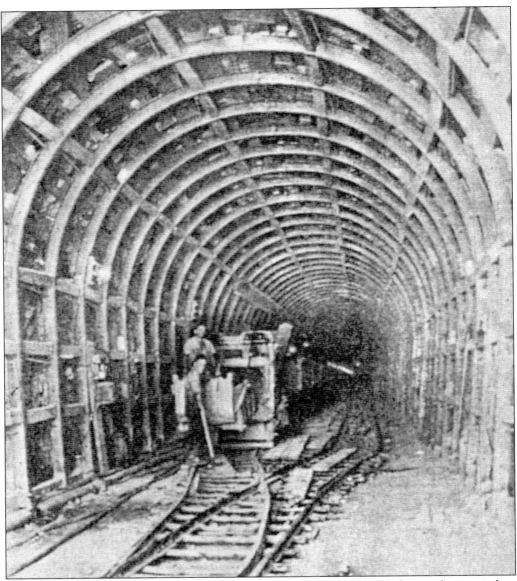

With remarkable foresight, the Metropolitan Water District planners designed an aqueduct adequate for future water needs. The huge 20-foot-diameter tunnels and pipeline would only be used to partial capacity in the 1940s and 1950s, but they foresaw the potential growth of Southern California and built accordingly. Youngstown, Ohio, rejoiced with Indio in 1935 when the Metropolitan Water District ordered the equivalent of the nation's entire production of steel for five months. A front-page article stated that the order for steel pipe sent to Indio helped take 8,000 off the charity rolls in Youngstown in June alone. The local newspaper reported that an immense steel welding plant had been set up at the Metropolitan Water District freight yard. It was working two shifts of 20 men each and was expected to put on another shift soon.

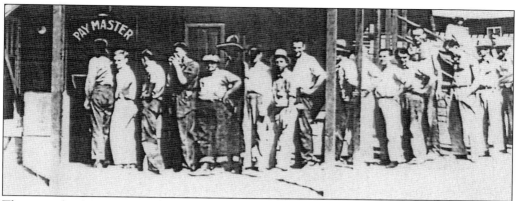

This is payday for some of the men lucky enough to get a job during the Depression. To be eligible to work on the project, they were supposed to be residents of one of the cities in the Metropolitan Water District, but there were ways around the rule. Berdoo Camp was just six miles east of Indio, and the men from this and other camps flocked into town on weekends.

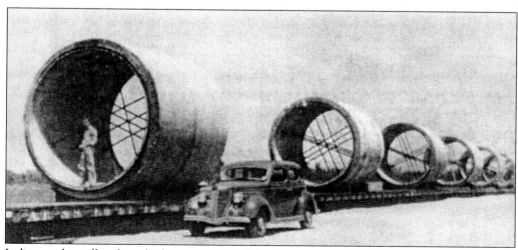

Indio was the railhead to which components of the immense aqueduct were delivered. These huge, pre-cast, concrete pipe sections were joined to form the siphons and portions of the aqueduct that were above ground.

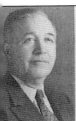 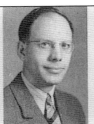 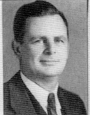 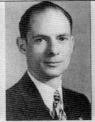 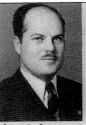 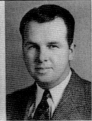 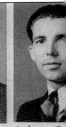

rle C. Taylor   F.B. Dozier   Art M. Westerfield   Eugene Jarvis   Clair S. Johnson   Fred H. Paine   Delano G

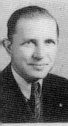 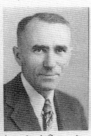 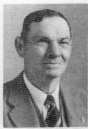 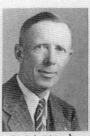

D. Dickey   Leonhart Swingle   S.C. McPheeters   Ralph Wool

1938
LIONS CLUB
Coachella Valley, California

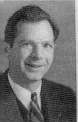 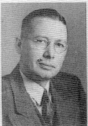 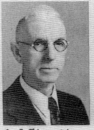 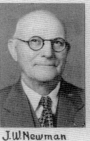 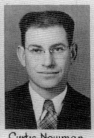 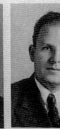

Ralph Roblee   George Berry   Rufus Choate   A.J. Shamblin   J.W. Newman   Curtis Newman   E. Keith F

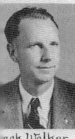 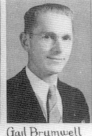 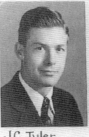 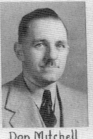 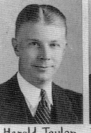 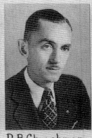 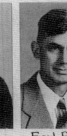

ack Walker   Gail Brumwell   J.C. Tyler   Don Mitchell   Harold Taylor   P.B. Churchman   Earl B

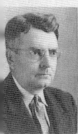 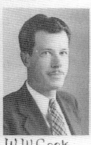 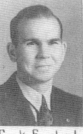 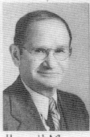 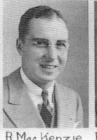 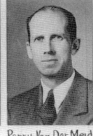 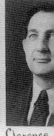

nn G. Jenkins   W.W. Cook   Frank Freeland   Harry H. Moore   R. MacKenzie   Perry Van Der Meid   Clarence

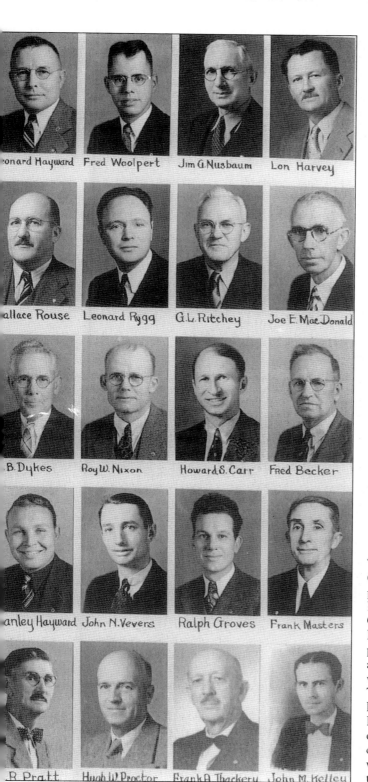

This 1938 photograph of the Coachella Valley Lions Club pictures many of Indio's civic leaders, as well as men from Coachella, Thermal, and Mecca. They welcomed the prosperity brought by the aqueduct project and coped with its new set of problems. The newspaper reported on Lions Club meetings held at the Berdoo Camp, where members enjoyed both the food and the opportunity to learn about the work. There were also dances to which locals were invited.

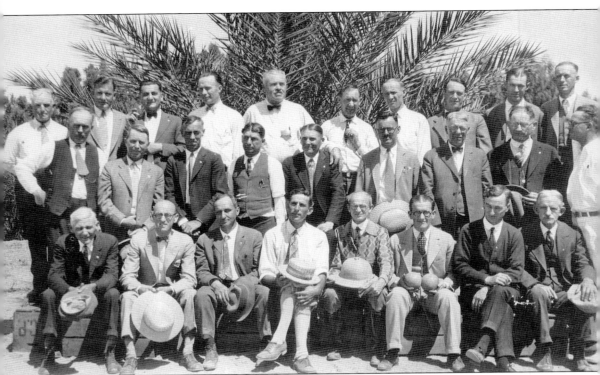

Before the 1930s, Indio's leading citizens had organized the Exchange Club, shown in this 1927 photograph. They included merchants and professional men—such men as Tim Coleman, Tom Allen, Knox Cologne, Felix Damien, H. W. Smiley, Marshall Peters, Ralph Sikes, and E. G. Shephard. They experienced the growth predicted in a 1933 newspaper article that said, "Indio will grow into a city of 10,000 people within the next few years." With remarkable accuracy, the writer wrote that the growth brought on by the aqueduct work would continue steadily and permanently, and concluded, "The 'back-country' of Los Angeles will become the playground and recreational country for the coast cities."

Five

WORLD WAR II CHANGED INDIO

Even before the United States entered World War II, military strategists anticipated their involvement in the conflict and began planning for waging war in the deserts of North Africa. Gen. George Patton (pictured right) was convinced that tanks would be the most effective weapons in that environment, and he personally selected a 162,000-acre site east of Indio to train troops for the North African campaign. The headquarters was named Camp Young, and it received its first 8,000 trainees in the spring of 1942. Patton himself only remained at Camp Young for about six months. On July 30, 1942, he received a telephone call from Gen. George Marshall in Washington, D.C. It was critical that the Axis's North African campaign be stopped before it reached the Suez Canal, and Patton's desert fighters were called to take action immediately. On November 8, 1942, Patton's forces landed on the French Moroccan coast. Indio was the closest town to Camp Young, and it prepared for its own invasion.

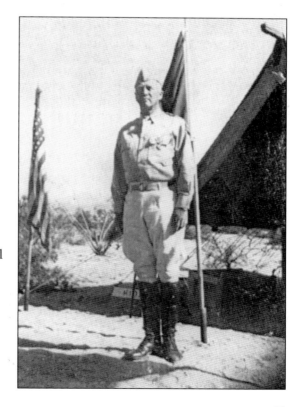

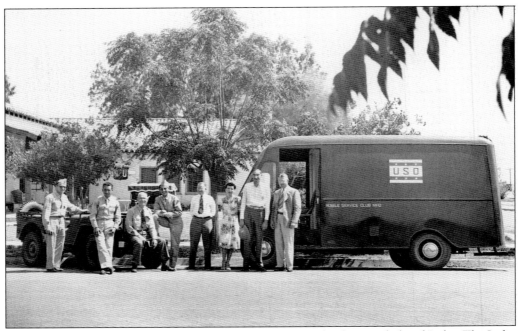

Soldiers were given leaves in groups of 2,500, and they completely overwhelmed Indio. The Indio Woman's Clubhouse became the USO, and local citizens provided services and a welcome. In the top photograph, Harold Taylor (on the right), assisted by Ora Jared from the Woman's Club, worked with the military. There were too few local girls to act as hostesses and dance partners, so girls came by bus from the Los Angeles area for special events.

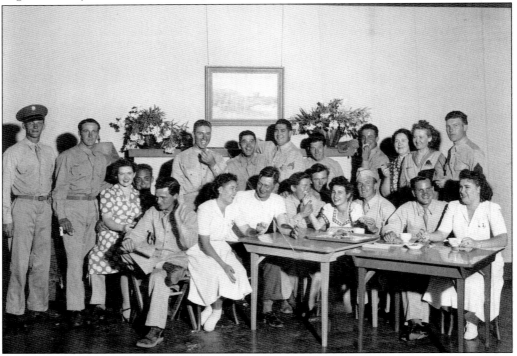

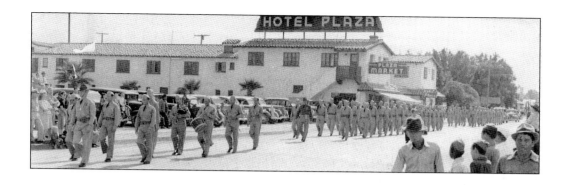

Troops were a familiar sight on Indio's streets during the war, often participating in local parades. The Hotel Plaza was noted for its prime rib dinners, but during the war, meat was scarce. If a soldier wanted a meal away from the base, he could sign for uncooked and canned food, and bring it to his favorite Indio café and have it prepared for him on the spot. Members of Indio's Civil Defense Committee are pictured in the lower photograph.

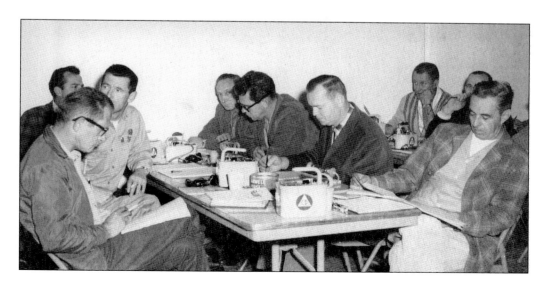

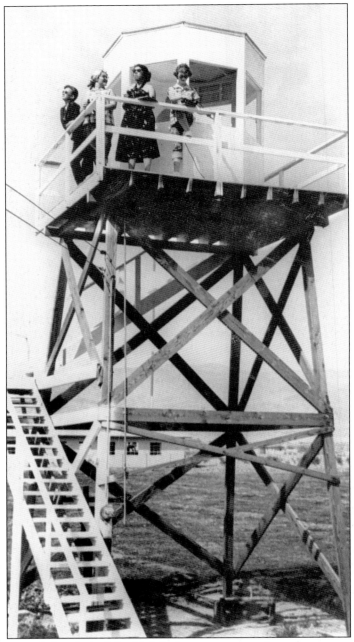

Indio's citizen's responded to the call for Civil Defense spotters, and watchtowers were built in Indio and other valley communities. As was the case in cities across the country, citizens worked with the Red Cross. Their biggest contribution, however, was the generous spirit exhibited toward the soldiers and their wives and children. Such a small town was in no way prepared for an invasion of 25,000 men and their families. People opened their homes, rented out spare bedrooms, and gave up trying to patronize merchants and entertainment venues when the troops came to town. Many of these servicemen returned to the valley after the war, appreciating the friendliness of the people.

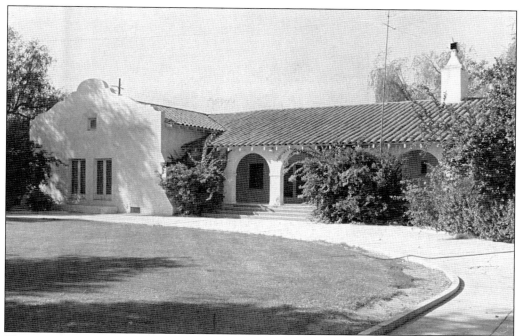

This interesting Mission-style home, located at the corner of Jackson Street and Avenue 48, has gained fame in recent days as the "Patton House." It was originally a part of the Whittier Ranch and was apparently rented to the Pattons for a brief period when Beatrice Patton joined her husband in Indio. Patton did participate in Indio's civic affairs and gave a Memorial Day address in 1942. He tried to lessen the impact of his troops' presence on the city. Many of his meetings took place in the Hotel Indio, shown below.

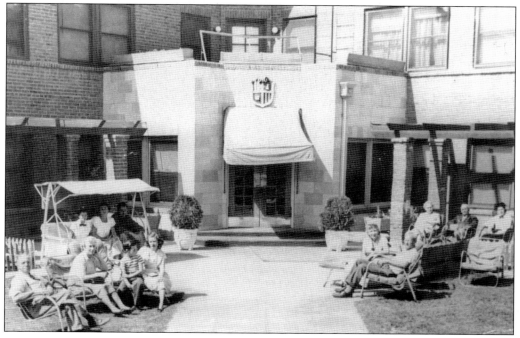

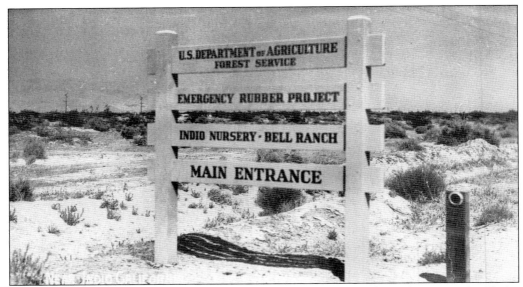

One of the war's great agricultural experiments took place on the Bell Ranch, just north of Indio on Highway 99. Called the "Emergency Rubber Project," it involved a large nursery of guayule plants, and it was hoped that the sap could be used to make synthetic rubber for the war effort. The results were disappointing. In the lower picture, Harold Taylor, manager of the Indio Bank of America; Tom Mullan, assistant manager; and Jackie Cochran are pictured in the second row from left to right. The bank handled payrolls that totaled $2 to 3 million each month for the desert training center. Money came by registered mail in bags two feet square and three feet high. It had to be counted by the bank and shipped to Camp Young under military escort, which included an airplane overhead.

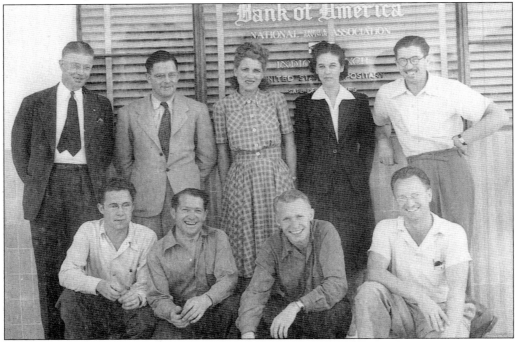

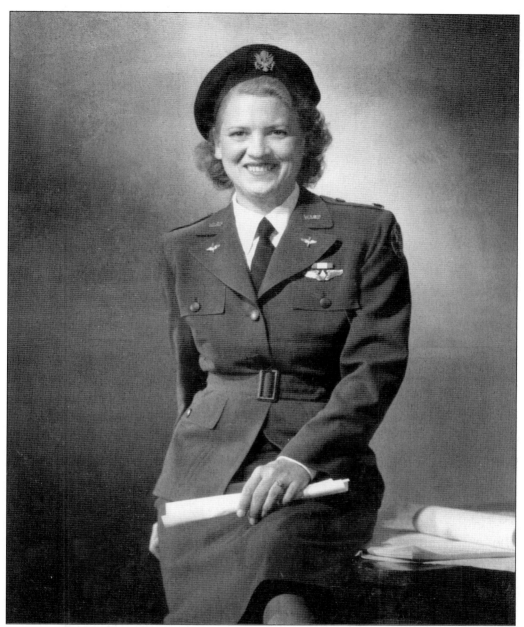

Jacqueline Cochran is probably the valley's most famous World War II service person. As an experienced pilot herself, she organized and directed the Women's Air Force Service Pilots, known as the WASPS. Over 1,000 women pilots ferried airplanes across the Atlantic and around the country, freeing men for combat duty. Female pilots were deactivated in 1944, but Cochran continued to serve as a consultant to the U.S. Army Air Force. The one-square-mile Indian Palms Country Club property on Monroe Street in Indio was her home. In 1946, she built the second golf course in the valley on her property.

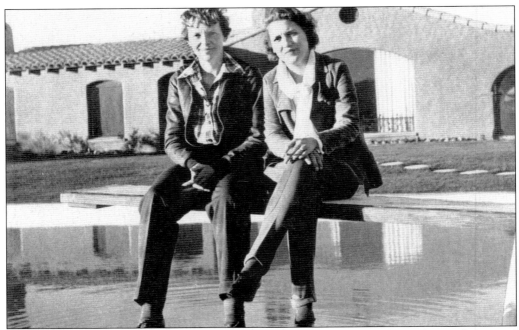

Jacqueline Cochran's passion for flying put her in contact with Amelia Earhart, who visited Cochran in the 1930s. Earhart spent time in the valley just prior to the ill-fated 1937 flight that ended in her disappearance in the South Pacific. Apparently, Cochran advised against the trip. Although now a part of the city of Indio, in the 1940s, the ranch was reported as being "three miles south of Indio" by the local newspaper.

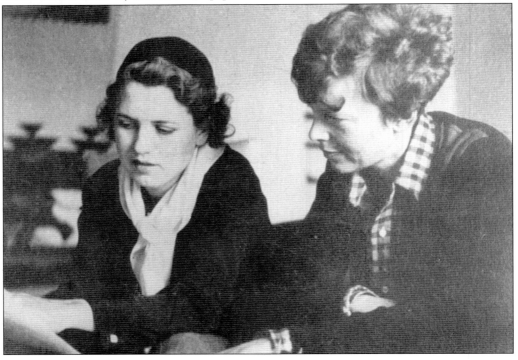

Not only did Jacqueline Cochran perform an unusual and important service during and after World War II, but her husband, industrialist Floyd Odlum, was recognized by Pres. Harry Truman with this Certificate of Merit. As founder of the Atlas Corporation, he made possible the construction of the Atlas missile and was instrumental in providing uranium for the nuclear projects. Odlum is shown on the right with his ranch manager, William Kersteiner. He is about to leave for his office in New York City aboard his private plane.

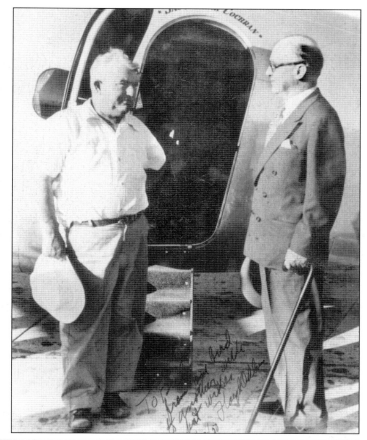

THE UNITED STATES OF AMERICA

TO ALL WHO SHALL SEE THESE PRESENTS, GREETING:

THE PRESIDENT OF THE UNITED STATES OF AMERICA
AWARDS THIS

CERTIFICATE OF MERIT

TO

FLOYD B. ODLUM

FOR OUTSTANDING FIDELITY AND MERITORIOUS CONDUCT
IN AID OF THE WAR EFFORT AGAINST THE COMMON
ENEMIES OF THE UNITED STATES AND ITS ALLIES
IN WORLD WAR II

GIVEN UNDER MY HAND IN THE CITY OF WASHINGTON
THIS SIXTEENTH DAY OF JULY 1947

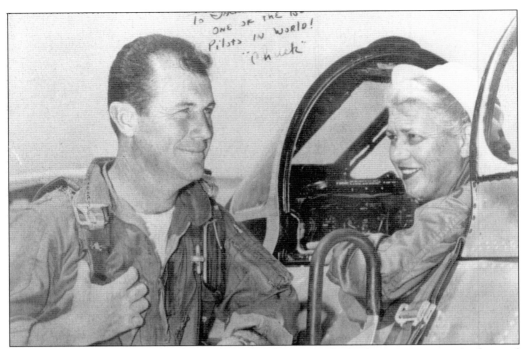

Jacqueline Cochran brought fame to Indio after the war as she broke one aviation speed record after another. Mentored by her friend, Chuck Yeager, she became the first woman to fly faster than the speed of sound. She used military planes at Edwards Air Force Base for the tests, but she kept her own plane at the Thermal Airport and flew back home after each test flight.

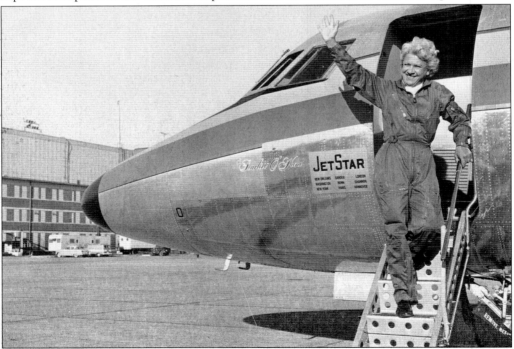

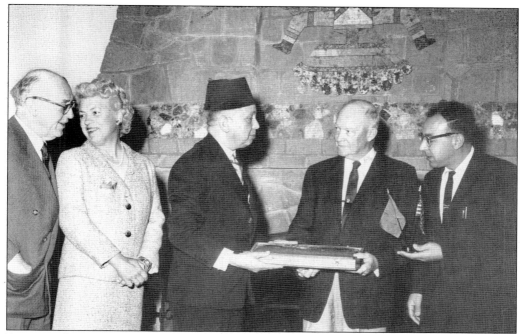

Pres. Dwight Eisenhower had an office at the Cochran-Odlum ranch after his retirement. He wrote a portion of his memoirs there and was a frequent social guest with his wife, Mamie. Floyd Odlum and his wife, Jacqueline Cochran, are on the left, as the Pasha of Kenitra makes a presentation in front of the ranch fireplace. The pasha was amazed that a former president of the United States would greet him personally at Thermal Airport. There were many famous "drop-in" guests brought to the Indio area by the hospitality offered at the ranch.

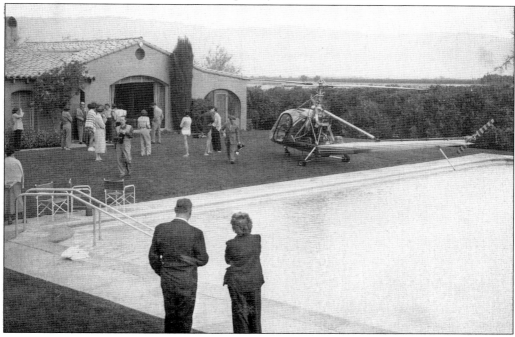

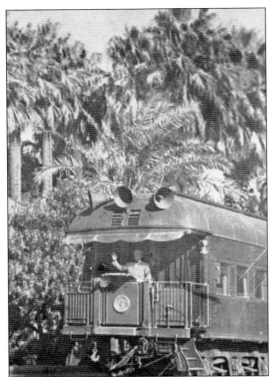

The Indio railroad depot saw several persons of national stature make it a whistle stop. Pres. Harry Truman waved and spoke to the Indio crowd on his way through town in 1948. Gov. Earl Warren and his wife and daughter are pictured below in front of the depot in 1951.

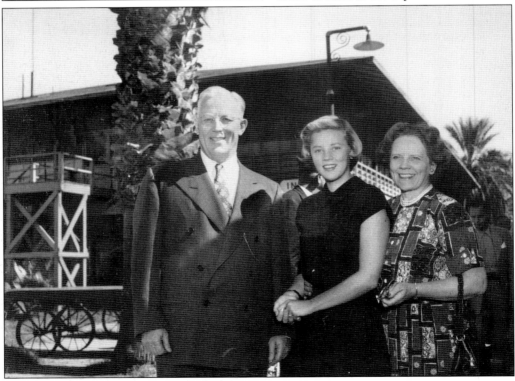

Six

WATER SHAPED DEVELOPMENT

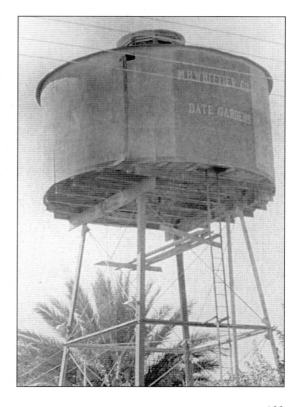

It has been said that "the power of water is greater than that of gold and silver." Nowhere is that more true than in the Coachella Valley. Finding that they could pump water from an underground aquifer, people came to Indio before 1900, but it was the deeper wells the railroad drilled that guaranteed continued development. Water was pumped into large water tanks, like this one from the Whittier Ranch on Indio's southern border, then was allowed to flow by gravity to water crops and supply domestic needs. By 1916, however, the water level in wells was dropping, and it was obvious that supplemental water would be needed if the growth of Indio and the valley were to continue. The Coachella Valley Water District was formed in 1918 to determine the capacity of the aquifer, to look for a source of supplemental water, and to control desert floods. It was a remarkably farsighted move. The Whittier Ranch tank is now located on the grounds of the Coachella Valley Historical Society museum on Miles Avenue in Indio.

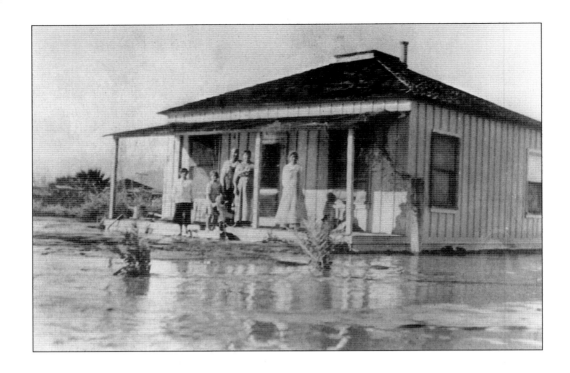

Most ranches had reservoirs that not only saved the water that often flowed from artesian wells in the early days, but also provided swimming pools for valley children and their parents. Needless to say, these ponds were very popular during the hot summers. Floodwaters were a problem, however. A storm in the mountains often sent flash floods clear to the center of the valley.

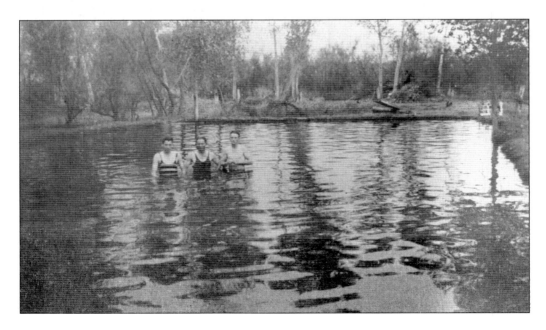

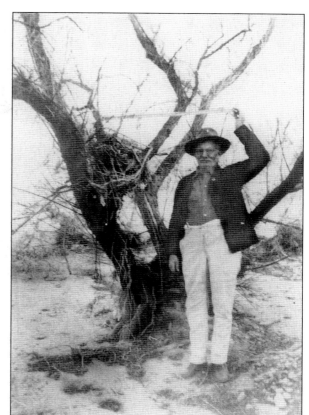

J. Win Wilson, editor of the *Date Palm* newspaper, measures the high water mark of a recent flood coming out of Box Canyon. There was controversy over the route for a new road to Blythe, and possible flooding was a consideration. Indio was hit with successive floods like this 1916 event shown below, which inundated the business district and isolated homes.

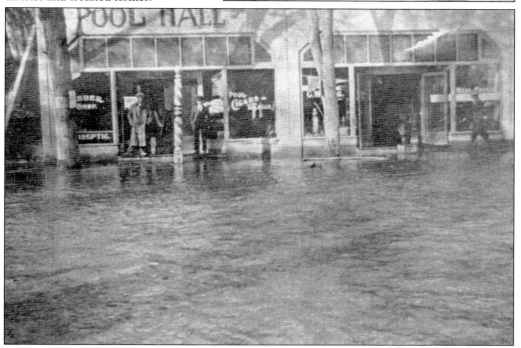

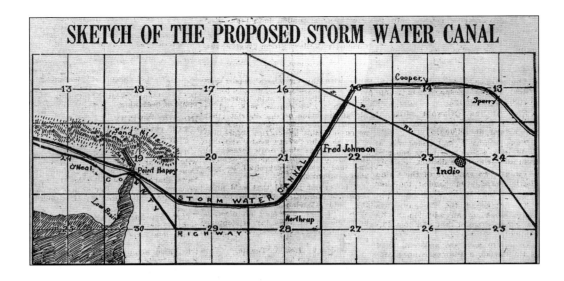

On August 30, 1918, the above sketch of the proposed Storm Water Canal appeared in the local newspaper. The article announced the upcoming election on September 14 to vote on a bond issue to cover the cost of taking care of storm water. At that time, there was no defined channel east of Point Happy, and water spread out all over Indio, surrounding farmland and cities to the east. Work was begun, but the lower photograph shows the 1927 flood racing south along Highway 99 north of Indio.

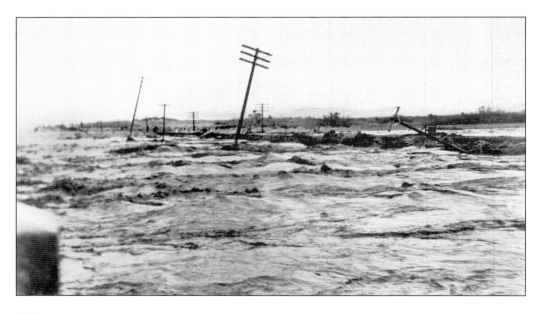

Usually there was no rain in Indio when the torrents of flood water rushed into town, flooding streets and cutting off both the highway and the railroad for hours and sometimes days. Summer rains in the mountains were the culprit. These pictures taken in 1938 on Fargo Street illustrate the problem. The movie showing at the Desert Theater is *The Rains Came*. The theater owner denied having anything to do with the weather!

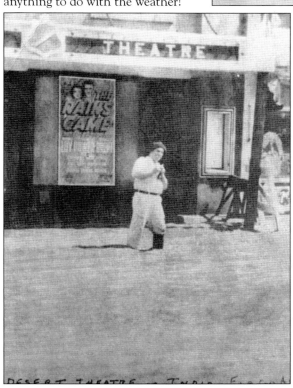

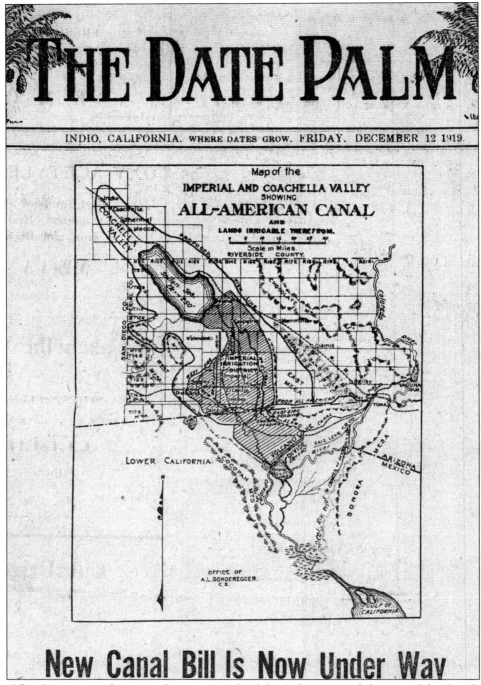

Brief floods were no solution to the water needs of the Indio area and the rest of the Coachella Valley. This front-page article in the December 12, 1919, issue of the Indio newspaper promised residents that Pres. Woodrow Wilson's Congress was working on legislation which would authorize construction of a dam on the Colorado River and a canal completely within the United States to deliver water to California's desert areas. Years of legislative arguments would ensue.

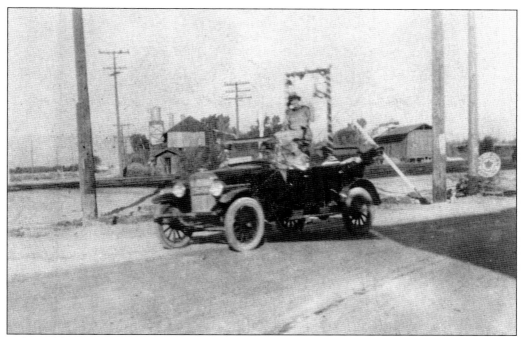

Indio residents joined the rest of the Coachella and Imperial Valley in pressing Congress for the All-American Canal project, which would bring Colorado River water to the desert. "Swing with Swing" was the slogan advertised by a local girl on a swing in this 1920s automobile. Congressman Phil Swing coauthored the legislation that authorized Bolder Dam and the canal. World War II delayed completion of the Coachella Branch of the All-American Canal, and the supplemental water did not reach the valley until 1948, but the land boom began immediately thereafter.

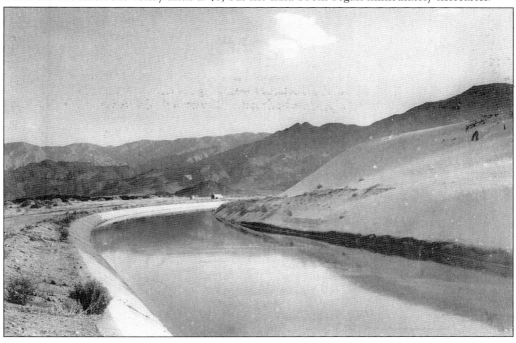

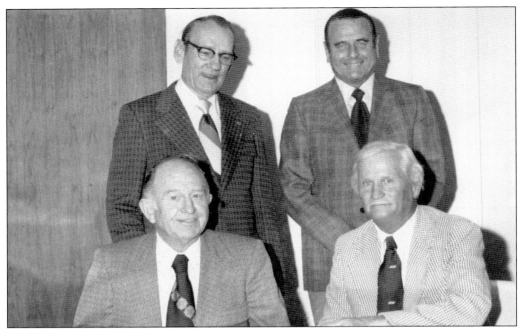

The U.S. Bureau of Reclamation was in charge of building the canal and its distribution system, but it was turned over to the Coachella Valley Water District upon completion. Pictured above, from left to right, are (first row) Lowell Weeks and Walter Wright; (second row) Ole Nordland and Maurice Sherrill. They deserve much of credit for managing this project that was so vital to the growth of Indio and the valley. Located southwest of Indio, the terminal reservoir of the canal, Lake Cahuilla, is a popular recreation spot, as well as a means to regulate water usage throughout the district's service area. Nordland was editor of the Indio newspaper for years before joining the water district staff.

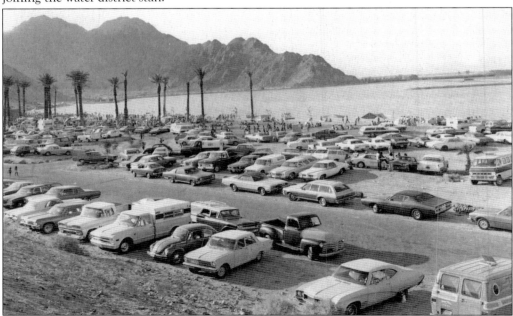

Seven
PARADES, PAGEANTS, FESTIVALS, AND FUN

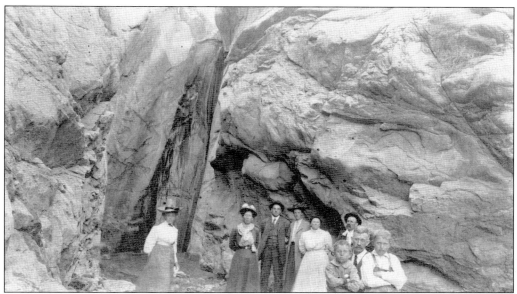

From the earliest days of settlement, Indio's residents shared each other's company and created as much enjoyment as was possible without the entertainment available in older communities. Picnics in the surrounding canyons were popular, as is shown in this 1909 snapshot of a picnic "at a waterfall in a canyon near Coral Reef." Coral Reef is on the west side of the valley near present-day PGA West. Almost everyone had a horse or pony and a wagon or buggy. This was really the best way to get across the sand dunes and rocky washes. The scenery was spectacular, and except for the middle of the summer, the weather was very pleasant. As the population grew, so did the opportunities for having fun. This chapter will share a few of them.

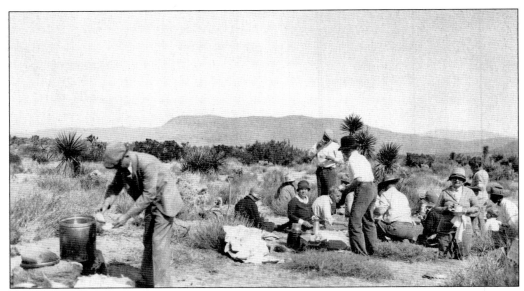
These 1929 picnickers ventured farther afield. The caption reads, "Taken in Berdoo canyon at Jackson Pass on Sunday, March 17, 1929." Berdoo Canyon is on the east side of the valley.

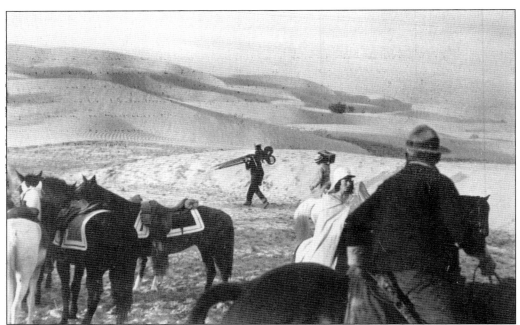
Not only did locals appreciate the desert scenery, but Hollywood had also discovered that they could use the valley as the setting for filming stories set in exotic places around the world. The oases in the eastern mountains, within sight of Indio, were used for movies such as *Tripoli, Ten Tall Men, Son of the Sheik, The Silver Chalice,* and *King of Kings.*

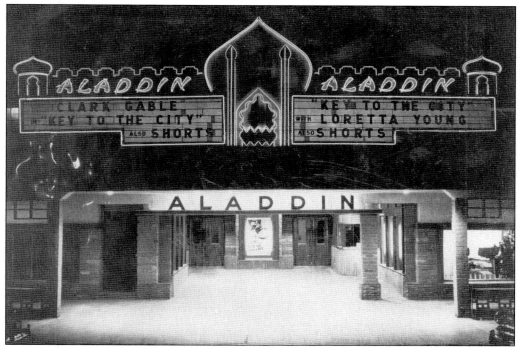

The Aladdin Theater was Indio's pride and joy when it opened in June 1948. It was far more elegant than the several smaller theaters that had preceded it.

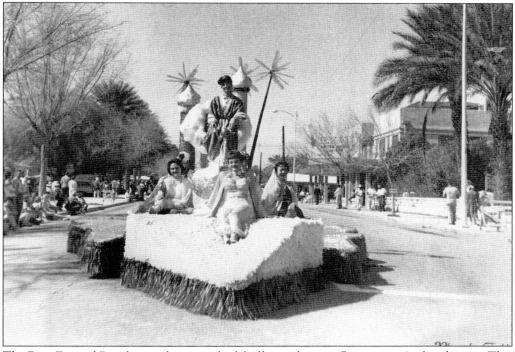

The Date Festival Parade was always a colorful affair with many floats using Arabic themes. This 1963 parade entry is shown passing the Aladdin Theater on the right.

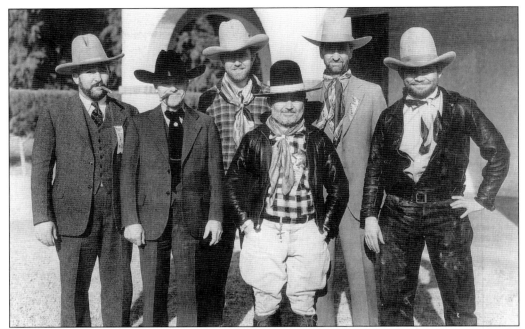

Western Days celebrations were popular in the late 1930s and 1940s. In the top photograph, the Indio Civic Club poses in front of the city hall in 1937. Members shown, from left to right, are Wallace Rouse, A. Rolland, Frank Purcell, F. Tebo, Clarence Washburn, and Hugh Moore. The club disbanded in 1946. In the lower photograph are, from left to right, Sherman Ohlhausen, David Goldie, Virgil Wicker, Pete Insolo, Frank Larro, Milton McCarroll, and E. W. (Ted) Johnston. Note the Shell gas pumps.

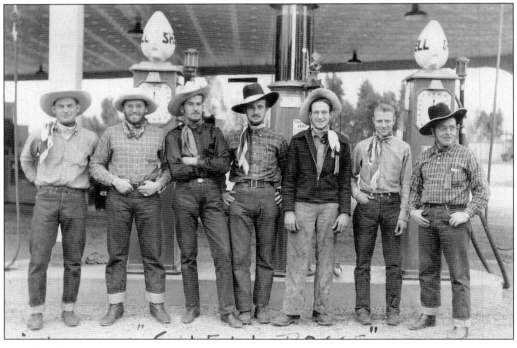

George Boomer (right) came to Indio in May 1920, in the employ of the Southern Pacific Railroad. He and his fellow railroad workers took a prominent part in Indio's civic affairs, including the celebration of Western Days. Judging from this picture, however, he managed to evade the posse on the lookout for anyone without whiskers. Movie stars loved the desert then, as now, and actor Jackie Cooper led the Indio parade in 1940, as shown in the lower photograph.

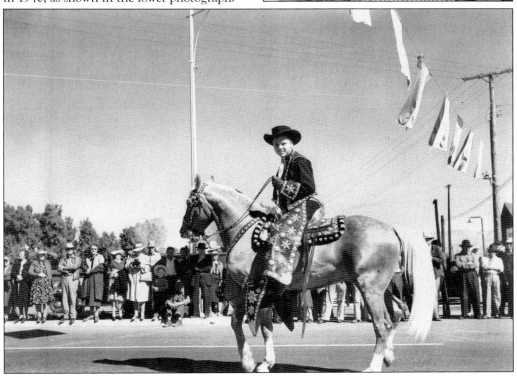

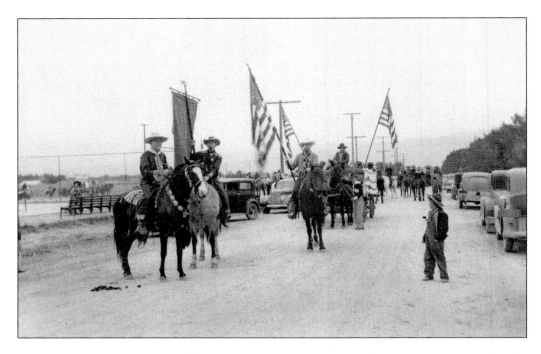

In this 1938 photograph, the Indio sheriff's posse lines up on Deglet Noor Street, just off Miles Avenue. The tennis court in the Miles Avenue Park is visible behind the first riders. The home of Dr. Smiley, one of Indio's first resident physicians, is on the right. It is now the site of the Coachella Valley Museum and Cultural Center. In the lower photograph, the 1939 parade makes its way down Fargo Street, having just turned the corner from Miles Avenue.

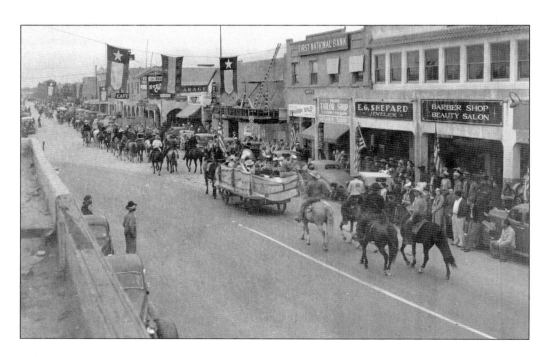

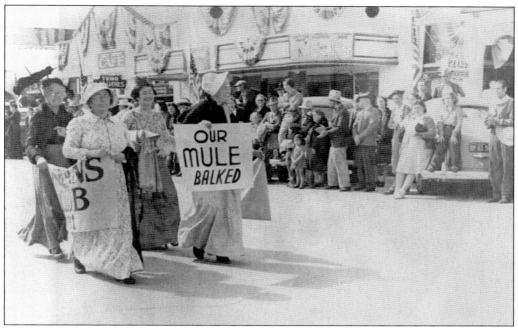

The Indio Woman's Club was not to be outdone. The ladies marched to publicize the many civic projects for which they were responsible. Dr. June Robertson McCarroll, single-handedly responsible for the valley's health care in the early years, carries the small umbrella.

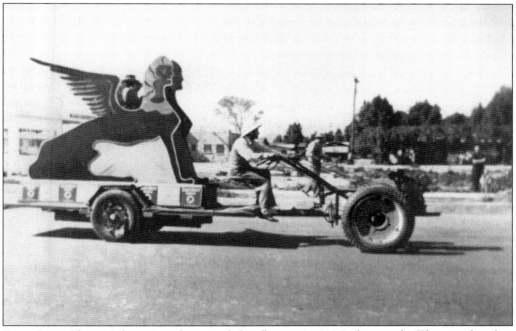

Zane Grey's Flying Sphinx Ranch entered this float in a 1939 Indio parade. The noted author was the owner of a ranch in the Oasis area being developed for him by Walter Pulsifer. The emblem was the seal of the ranch, taken from the World War I flying squadron of Grey's friend, Earl B. Wallace.

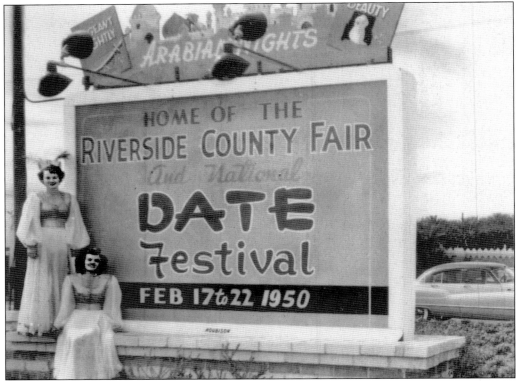

The annual Riverside County Fair and National Date Festival became a civic event the entire community took part in. After the first fairs in 1921 and 1922, the celebration was not repeated until 1941, when the fair was held in a huge tent. Ground was broken for permanent buildings in the fall of 1941. The Indio Civic Club spearheaded the effort to get the county to pay $10,000 for the 40-acre site where the fairgrounds and county buildings are located. City council members ride proudly in the first cars of the 1948 Date Festival parade.

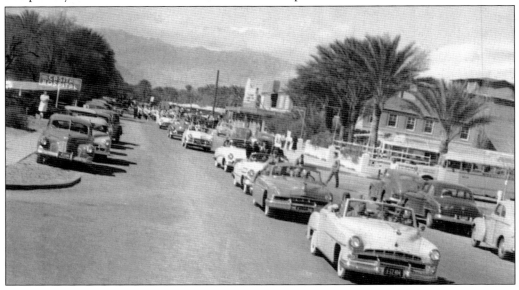

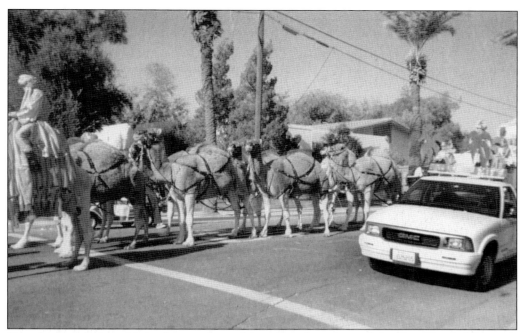

Camels were always a hit in the parades and in the performances of the Date Festival Pageant. Indio's municipal band furnished not only a float, but also music for this undated date festival photograph. The parade has just turned the corner from Miles Avenue onto Oasis Street. Note the Auto Club of Southern California office in the background. Bob Williams's men's store was on the left. (Below, courtesy of the Indio Chamber of Commerce.)

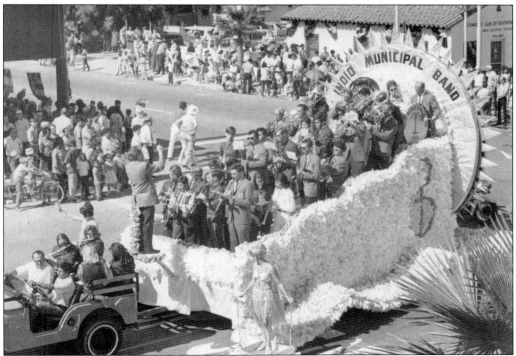

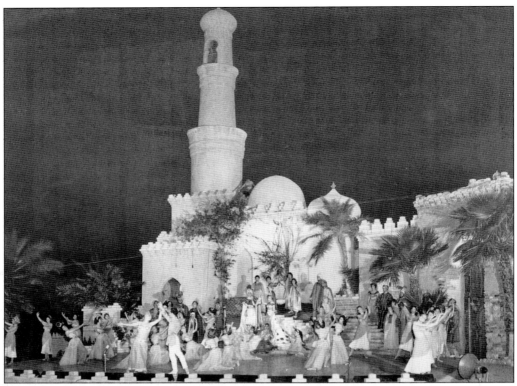

In 1947, an Arabian theme was officially adopted for the spectacular evening pageant performed nightly during the annual 10-day run of the National Date Festival. An elaborate permanent stage was constructed under the direction of Harry Oliver, an experienced builder of sets for the movie industry. Most of the performers are local residents, although lead roles have sometimes been played by professionals. The Date Festival's February date is determined by the California State Fair schedule. Costuming, lighting, and music make it a highlight of fair attendance. Each year, a new script is used for the pageant, usually written by someone locally. The dramatic permanent stage, reminiscent of an Oriental marketplace and a caliph's palace, lends itself well to adaptations of the Arabian Nights' tales.

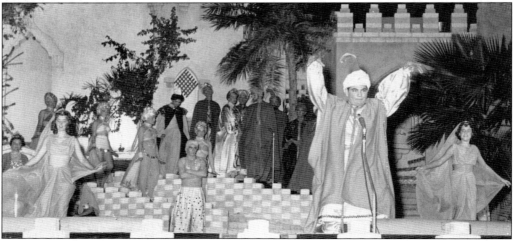

Pictured from left to right are (first row) Dorothy Gavin and Ruth Sorenson; (second row) Sonny Silva, Eva Claiborne, and Bill Wool. All five were members of the Pageant Board who served for years, planning and appearing in the yearly production.

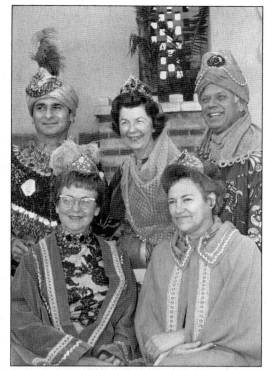

The Date Festival's main exhibit hall is called the Taj Mahal and features mainly dates and other agricultural products. Growers and date shop owners compete for prizes. These two "princesses" call attention to one of the beautifully packed trays of dates.

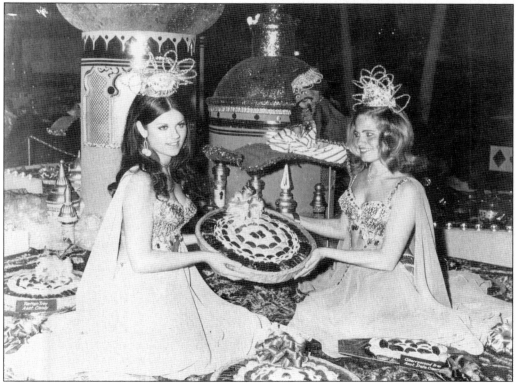

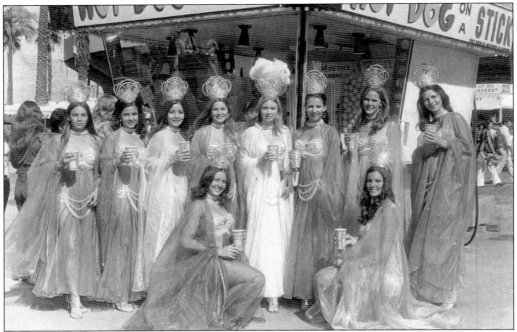

Queen Scheherazade and her court were the official hostesses for the fair. Their colorful costumes made them favorite subjects for camera-carrying fans, and they graciously posed for group photographs and singly with family groups. Originally, each city in Riverside County nominated a girl to represent them, and one of those girls was selected as queen. In later years, just five or six girls were selected from throughout the county. In the lower photograph, the queen and several of her princesses pose with the Indio Chamber of Commerce feature display in the Taj Mahal.

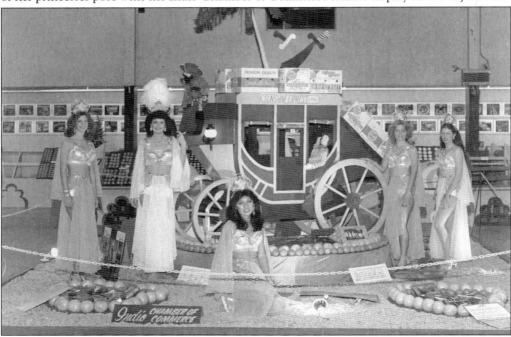

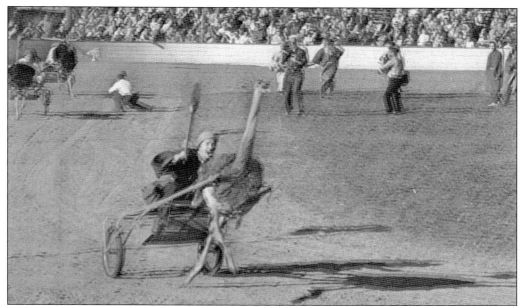

The Date Festival Pageant elaborated on the original "Thousand and One Nights" theme and used interesting animals in walk-on roles in the performances. During the daytime, however, the same animals entertained fairgoers by participating in the always-popular ostrich and camel races, and providing rides for visitors. The top photograph is an action shot of an ostrich race in the horse show arena. In the right photograph, the queen and two of her princesses chose to pose on a good-looking elephant.

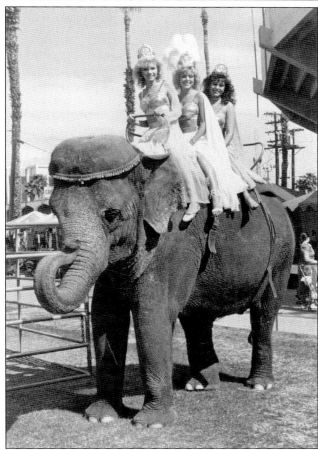

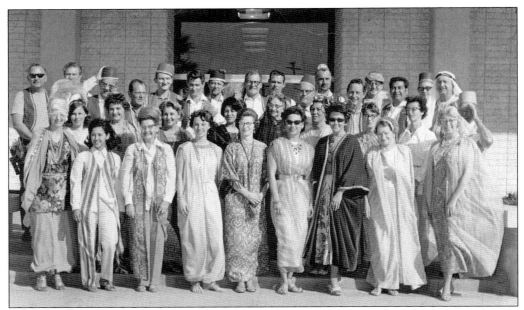

This 1978 photograph of all the employees working at the Riverside County Office Building in Indio is evidence of the support the community gave to the Date Festival. Nearly every business encouraged its workers to dress in a version of Arabic costume, and local fairgoers were sold a reduced-price ticket if they came in costume. It added greatly to the atmosphere. As Indio and the valley grew, Riverside County built a much larger courthouse with additional offices.

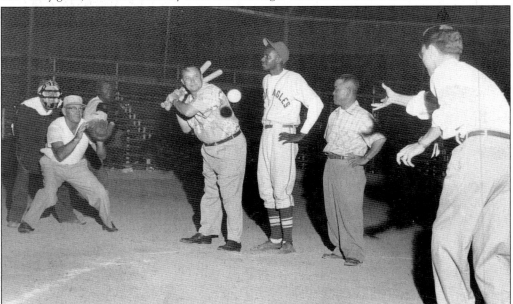

Indio was part of an active Coachella Valley Recreation District, and there were many sports opportunities. Swimming was especially popular during the hot summer months at the Pawley and North Indio pools, but there was a lot of interest in baseball. In this photograph of the opening of the 1955 summer softball season, Mayor Gordon Cologne throws out the first pitch to batter Kay Olesen. One of the onlookers is Fred Okamoto, third in line behind the batter.

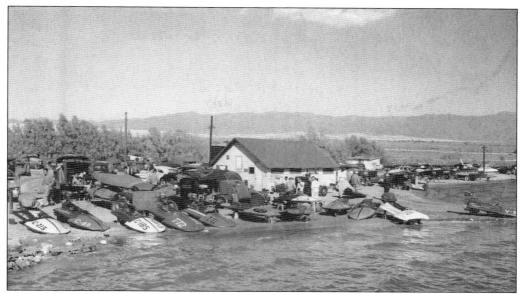

The Salton Sea attracted water skiers, swimmers, and, particularly, speedboat enthusiasts. Low barometric pressure and greater water density made the sea one of the fastest bodies of water in the world, and many records were set here in the late 1940s and early 1950s. Thousands flocked to the sea to see the powerful boats owned by Henry J. Kaiser and Horace Dodge, as well as the small speedboats shown in this photograph.

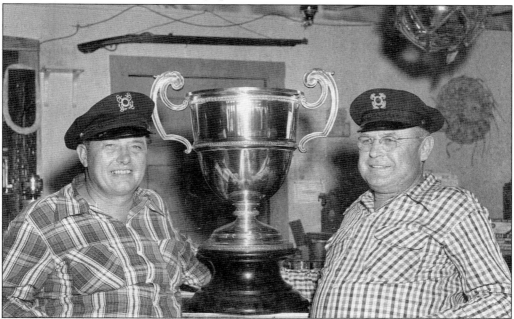

Indio merchants sponsored races and provided trophies to winners. The Indio Jaycees were among its strongest local supporters. In this photograph, the same Kay Olesen who played summer softball stands on the left of the impressive trophy awarded to the Gold Cup winner. In this particular year, the boat *Black Jack* defeated the Canadian national champion from Ontario. On the right is Glenn Gurley, another Indio merchant active in staging the races.

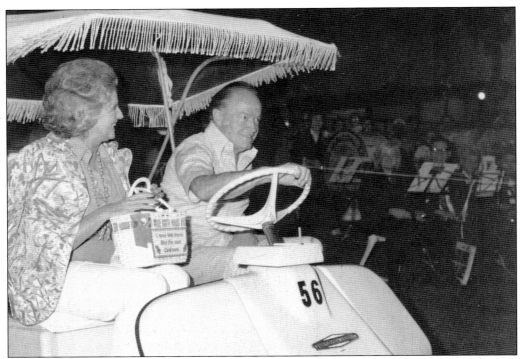

No story about fun in Indio would be complete without mentioning golf. The second golf course to be built in the valley was the Cochran Ranch course, now called Indian Palms. Indio built its own par-three course north of I-10, and Bob and Dolores Hope became good neighbors who showed up at a fund-raiser for the Municipal Golf Course.

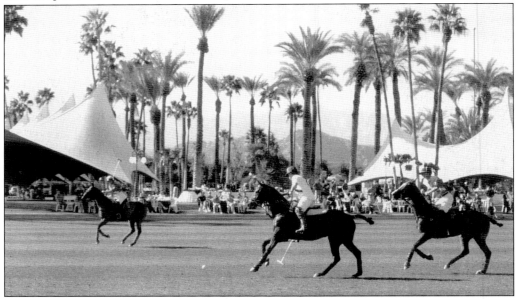

Polo has put Indio on the map in recent years. Both the Empire Polo Club and the Eldorado Polo Club have brought leading polo players and their horses to these venues on Indio's south border. Most recently, outstanding music festivals have been held here as well.

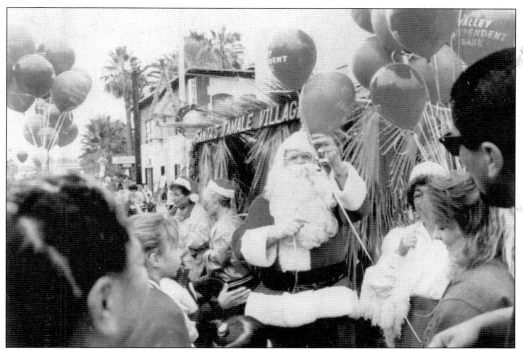

Two views show Indio's very popular Tamale Festival. Held in early December, it attracts more than 100 vendors selling their special tamales. Street dancing and other entertainment are featured. Calling on the culture of its many Hispanic residents, the city has also begun holding a Salsa Festival annually. It truly is a "City of Festivals." (Both, courtesy of the Indio Chamber of Commerce.)

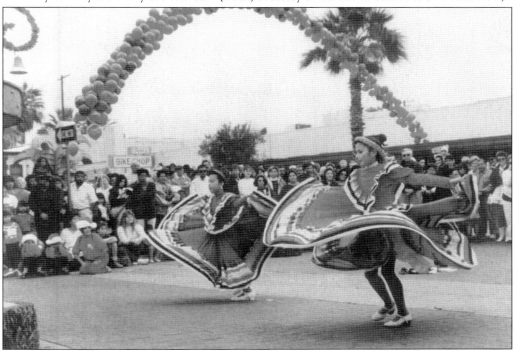

ACROSS AMERICA, PEOPLE ARE DISCOVERING SOMETHING WONDERFUL. *THEIR HERITAGE.*

Arcadia Publishing is the leading local history publisher in the United States. With more than 4,000 titles in print and hundreds of new titles released every year, Arcadia has extensive specialized experience chronicling the history of communities and celebrating America's hidden stories, bringing to life the people, places, and events from the past. To discover the history of other communities across the nation, please visit:

www.arcadiapublishing.com

Customized search tools allow you to find regional history books about the town where you grew up, the cities where your friends and family live, the town where your parents met, or even that retirement spot you've been dreaming about.

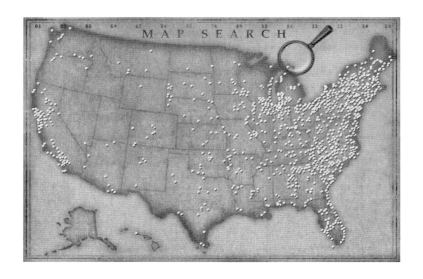